# SACHA BARON COHEN

*Unkindness of Ravens*

*Morgan Freeman: A Biography*

*Ellen: The Real Story of Ellen DeGeneres*

*Diana Rigg: The Biography*

*The Girl's Got Bite: The Original
Unauthorized Guide to Buffy's World*

*Angelina Jolie*

*Regis! The Unauthorized Biography*

*The Secret Story of Polygamy*

*Dixie Chicks*

*Daytime Divas: The Dish on Dozens
of Daytime TV's Great Ladies*

*Imus: A Biography*

*Jerry Seinfeld: The Entire Domain*

*The Boy Who Would Be King: An Intimate Portrait
of Elvis Presley by His Cousin*

KATHLEEN TRACY

# SACHA BARON COHEN

## THE UNAUTHORISED BIOGRAPHY

BOOKS

First published in Great Britain in 2008 by
JR Books, 10 Greenland Street, London NW1 0ND
www.jrbooks.com

ISBN 978-1-906217-46-4

1 3 5 7 9 10 8 6 4 2

Printed by MPG Books, Bodmin, Cornwall

**TO ZACH,**

FOR DRAGGING ME

TO SEE THE MOVIE

# CONTENTS

# CONTENTS

# ACKNOWLEDGMENTS

I would like to thank my editor, Elizabeth Beier, for her saint-like patience with deadline-challenged writers, and Michelle Richter for helping to guide me through the copyediting. A special thanks to Heather Huettl for both slogging through the permissions minefield and keeping me laughing.

# Who Is This *Guy?*

**SO** you **SAYING** God **made** da **world?** And SINCE then **he's JUST** **CHILLED?** —Ali G

**IN** the beginning, there was Ali G.

In 2000, HBO premiered the U.S. version of *Da Ali G Show,* a hybrid of improv, *The Daily Show,* and *Punk'd.* Unsuspecting guests, believing they were appearing on a legit talk show aimed at the hip-hop audience, found themselves at the mercy of an irreverent-bordering-on-rude host named Ali G, who would blithely expound politically incorrect views and observations. The show also featured special reports and interviews presented by a Kazakh reporter named Borat and by Bruno, a flamboyantly gay Austrian fashion correspondent.

Talking to everyone from Pat Buchanan and Boutros Boutros-Ghali to Shaquille O'Neal and David Beckham, Ali G and his cohorts did their best to get under the carefully polished public images and prepped answers. The results were often controversial, frequently adversarial, regularly cringe-worthy, surprisingly revealing—and undeniably entertaining. What could be more fun than seeing Andy Rooney kick Ali G out of his office in a sputtering snit?

Since 1998, Sacha Baron Cohen, in the guise of Ali G, had been popping the pompous bubbles of starchy politicians and posh intellectuals, making the gangsta wannabe a huge cultural phenomenon throughout the United Kingdom. How huge? Picture this. . . .

Not long after the Queen Mother's death in 2002, Princes William and Harry had a formal sit-down with the press to reminisce about their great-grandmother. While anecdotes about her feisty independence and playful nature brought a tear to the eye of royalists everywhere, a few brows were no doubt raised when her grandsons recounted the Queen Mum's off-the-cuff impersonation of Ali G.

The Windsor clan had gathered for their Christmas holiday at Sandringham, Queen Elizabeth's estate in northern Norfolk County, and the lads were watching *Da Ali G Show*.

"We were laughing when she came in," William recalled. "She couldn't understand what was going on, so we explained to her what he was doing. She saw Ali G click his fingers and say, 'Respec,' and Harry and I showed her what to do. She loved it, and after three goes she had it."

(That none of the cynical Fleet Street reporters asked why it took the beloved old gal three tries to get the sequence of 1. Snap fingers 2. Pause 3. Say the word "respect" with a faux Jamaican accent speaks to the solemnity of the occasion.)

Later that day, continued Prince Harry, the family was in the dining room having Christmas lunch. "It was at the end of the meal, and she stood up and said [to her daughter

Elizabeth], 'Darling, lunch was marvelous—respec,' and clicked her fingers."

The family burst out laughing at the hilarity of it—obviously, you had to be there—and even the Queen was reportedly amused. Considering that the Windsors have never been known as a laugh-a-minute monarchy (the late Princess Margaret's exploits aside), it's a testament to Baron Cohen's comedic gifts that his humor cut a swath across all classes of English society and elevated him to pop cultural icon status.

America, however, was another story. Although *Da Ali G Show* earned an Emmy nomination, except for HBO subscribers the program and its band of in-your-face characters remained largely under the mainstream radar in the States . . . until a movie named *Borat* became one of the most talked about comedies in recent memory. It may also end up being the most litigated film in Hollywood history as participants try to backpedal out of unguarded revelations of ignorant boorishness and self-involvement at best, racism and prejudice at worst.

But even now, the man behind the uproar remains largely an enigma. For much of Sacha Baron Cohen's career, he has preferred to let his fictional personas take center stage, as he remains in character for interviews and press functions. So just who is this social provocateur who turned an uncomfortable mirror on America's dark side, eliciting both laughter and introspection? How has he managed to dupe media-savvy politicians, pundits, and celebrities into being his unwitting foils on his near-quixotic quest to use humor to promote tolerance and understanding? What informs the performer who is willing to present a bag of fresh feces to his fellow dinner party guests (taking shits and giggles to a disturbingly literal extreme)? Is it courage? Crassness? Sociopathy?

Whether he is "our generation's Peter Sellers," as his friend and admirer Madonna gushed, or a one-trick pony, his is a unique approach to comedy, making Baron Cohen, at least for the moment, the heir apparent picking up the baton from the trail blazed before him by Lenny Bruce, Richard Pryor, and George Carlin. Anyone who manages to incite both sides of the political and social spectrum to riot—let's face it, how many people can say they've nearly been sued by a former Soviet Bloc country *and* Naomi Wolf?—must have substance as well as carefully manipulated style.

Over the years Baron Cohen has obsessively deflected glimpses into his life, and head, by keeping his characters front and center, as if the illusion were his talisman and letting the real Sacha show would destroy his creative mojo. But success and maturity have a way of relaxing defenses and Baron Cohen has been gradually emerging from his comedic cocoon, offering fans, critics, and the merely curious an opportunity to glean what truly makes Sacha run. And just like his characters, the answer is as unexpected as it is telling.

# 1

# Iz It Coz I'ze Welsh?

**AS** a **CHILD**, my dad **made** us **watch** American **SHOWS** he **loved** **GROWING** up, everything from *Sgt. BILKO* to **Sid Caesar's** *Your* **SHOW** *of* **SHOWS**. —SACHA Baron **COHEN**

**IT'S** ironic that the Borat and Ali G characters have been accused of being anti-Semitic, considering that Sacha Baron Cohen is Jewish. However, contrary to reports that he is devoutly Orthodox, Baron Cohen's identity is more firmly rooted in the secular.

"I wouldn't say I'm a religious Jew," he admits, explaining that his observances have more to do with Jewish cultural customs and traditions. When in England, for example, he'll spend Friday nights with his family and "we'll light the candles. A couple times a year I will go to synagogue." He also tries to keep kosher, not because he's religious, but "because I'm culturally and historically proud of my Jewish identity."

And that heritage he identifies with comes to him from two disparate lineages. Although the individual experiences for each side of his family tree differed, the reality of living with a bull's-eye on their back because of their faith merged into a collective consciousness that has left its indelible mark on each subsequent generation, in one fashion or another. For some of his relatives, it fueled the fires of commercial ambition; for Sacha, it informed his desire to expose passive prejudice through biting humor and seek understanding and tolerance through the laughter of recognition.

Whether any of his ancestors would find *Borat*'s running-of-the-Jews scene funny is debatable since there weren't a lot of yucks finding oneself an endangered species. Sacha's mother, Daniella Weiser, was born in Israel, the daughter of a German Jew whose girlhood dream of being a dancer was derailed by Hitler's rise to power.

"The Nazis were incredibly fair," Baron Cohen dead-pans, "because they had a rule that any Jew who enrolled [in school] before the Nuremberg laws was allowed to complete their education. Just no Jews afterward were allowed to. So [my grandmother] stayed until 1936 . . . and was basically the last Jewish girl taught ballet in Germany."

By that time, Sacha's paternal clan was long gone from the area, having joined the exodus of Jews fleeing the pogroms that had become increasingly common, and increasingly brutal, throughout Eastern Europe in the late nineteenth century. Sacha's great-grandfather Hyman Baron Cohen was among those who sought refuge in London. Broke and unable to speak English, he took whatever work was available. For immigrant Jews that usually meant a job in one of east London's notorious clothing sweatshops.

But the harsh circumstances became the backdrop for Hyman's courtship of coworker Amelia Angell, who had also come to London in search of tolerance and safety. The couple married and decided to make their home in Wales, which had a growing Jewish immigrant population of merchants and would-be entrepreneurs hoping to cash in on the influx of laborers from the Continent looking for work in coal mines and factories.

Eventually, anti-Semitism reared its head in Wales, and in August 1911 Jewish businesses in the south Wales coal-mine countryside were attacked by mobs, prompting most of the Jewish immigrants to leave and settle in Cardiff's Jewish ghetto along with five thousand others struggling to survive and somehow integrate into the local citizenry—not an easy task. Being Jewish in Wales is akin to being a snake-handling revival Baptist in Italy—to say you are a minority doesn't remotely begin to describe the cultural isolation Jewish immigrants in Wales faced.

"We were always outsiders," says Baron Cohen's uncle, Sammy Epstein, a retired film distribution manager who still lives in Cardiff. "Sacha is very mindful of his history. He is proud of his Jewish and Welsh roots, even though he once came down here and poked fun at the Welsh in one of his shows."

Hyman and Amelia settled near Cardiff and had fifteen children. Sacha's grandfather Morris, the second oldest of seven brothers, was born in 1900 in Pontypridd, which is also Tom "Panty Magnet" Jones's hometown. Tales of the hardships Morris and his siblings endured have become family lore.

**Pontypridd Bridge** *Courtesy of Wikipedia (www.wikipedia.com)*

Baron Cohen's cousin Samuel Minton reveals that Morris's family "lived in a hovel in a real ghetto" that had no electricity, no heat, no indoor plumbing, "and appalling hygiene." Food was scarce and hunger was common. Their home was so tiny, all the kids shared one bedroom. Hyman struggled to support his family by working as an all-around fix-it man who repaired everything from glass to pots and pans.

"It was an incredibly hard life," Epstein says. "They peddled services and were paid in installments." There were some suggestions among locals that Morris drummed up extra business by encouraging local youths to go around breaking windows so that he would be hired to repair them. That was the first clue young Morris had a bright future in business . . . or as Tony Soprano's director of marketing.

With money so scarce, education was a luxury Morris's family could not afford. When each kid turned fourteen, he or she had to quit school and find a job. "The girls became dressmakers," Epstein says, "while the boys did all sorts of menial work, selling glass and even going down the pits." Morris went to work when he was eleven, earning sixpence a week, or the equivalent of about twelve cents.

When World War I broke out, five of the Baron Cohen boys enlisted. "There was never any question about waiting to be called up," Sammy says. "They all went straightaway to volunteer. They felt one hundred percent British and wanted to fight for Britain."

Most of the Baron Cohen brothers lied about their age so they could be enlisted. Fourteen-year-old Morris— short, slight of build, and nearsighted—claimed to be nineteen and was assigned to the Cardiff City Battalion. He became the youngest non-commissioned British officer and saw combat in France, Germany, and Belgium. Three of his *younger* brothers also served.

Inordinately confident and mature, Morris went on to become a sergeant. "Well, he was always a noisy beggar," observes Sammy, "and obviously clever, with all his marbles about him."

The eldest Baron Cohen son, Isaac, was wounded at Ypres and died of pneumonia on the last day of the war. Morris took the responsibility of being the oldest living son to heart.

"Although he was only eighteen, Morris was the elder

statesman of the family, always on the go and a real go-getter," Epstein says. "He worked hard, he took menial jobs, anything he could find. . . . And he always did it with the most remarkable sense of humor."

For a while Morris followed his dad's lead and worked as a tinker. Being a resourceful young man, Morris frequently subsidized his meager earnings hustling at snooker. But as Europe's economy began the slide that would ultimately domino into the Great Depression, work became scarce in Wales. So Morris periodically traveled to London in hopes of finding a decent-paying job. Instead, he found a high-spirited Cockney maiden named Miriam. The couple married in 1929 and settled in London's Stepney neighborhood, not far from Whitechapel, where Jack the Ripper had roamed forty years earlier.

Miriam and Morris's two sons, Hymie and Gerald, were born in England, but Morris was homesick and moved his family back to Wales. He was hired at a tailor's store where he finally found his niche, turning the job into a thriving family business.

Alan Schwartz, who edited a Welsh Jewish publication called *Bimah,* recalled in a London *Daily Mail* interview that Morris "was a decent, strait-laced sort of bloke." Even though business and financial matters were his primary focus, Schwartz says Morris was also "fairly orthodox and observant to the faith and our holidays. He became a pillar of the community and was made the honorary warden of our local synagogue. . . . Morris liked to be known as a professional and his wife certainly lived up to it."

Another acquaintance recalls that Miriam was much more outgoing than her husband. "She was hilariously loud and ebullient and you could hear her coming a mile away." As Morris became more prosperous, Miriam nudged her husband to upgrade their lifestyle by moving to a posher neighborhood in Cardiff, "but she still insisted on shopping in the poorer part of town."

While Miriam was out looking for bargains, Morris did a mitzvah by establishing a scholarship for underprivileged children. He also set his sons up with their own tailoring company, called Morris Cowan, with outlets in Cardiff and London. Gerald moved to London in the 1960s.

Although Sacha's maternal grandmother still lived in Haifa, Israel, where she ran—and continues to run—a fitness center for geriatrics, Daniella had moved to London and supported herself as a movement instructor. After their marriage, she and Gerald settled in the well-heeled Hampstead Garden suburb, where they raised three sons.

Sacha Noam Baron Cohen was born on October 13, 1971, and grew up in the family's three-story redbrick house, the youngest child. His father owns the House of Baron clothier, located in always trendy Piccadilly. By all accounts Sacha's was a typical upper-middle-class upbringing—plenty of creature comforts, minimal money worries, and tacit parental expectations of achieving personal success.

As Sacha was growing up, the family consensus was that

he had inherited Grandma Miriam's outgoing humor, served with a splash of vermouth. In 1981, he wrote an essay about school that practically reeks of a precocious sarcasm: "My first lesson on Monday morning is English. This reminds us of the correct way to speak and write English. This is very important as most of the boys have been watching television and speaking with their parents all weekend."

Many years later he recounted a history lesson that detailed the life and times of people in the Stone Age, concluding that such knowledge would in the future help him and his peers to better survive "many bad English winters and strikes."

Maths was Baron Cohen's favorite subject because it offered the comfort of consistency in an otherwise always changing world. "Russia may have invaded Afghanistan, England may have lost against the West Indies at cricket, and the price of Smarties has jumped 5p. But in our maths lesson nothing has changed."

It's not too hard to see how the self-satisfied amusement expressed would eventually ferment into Baron Cohen's signature dry, sardonic wit.

All the Baron Cohen brothers attended the public, all-boy, apostrophe-heavy Haberdashers' Aske's Boys' School, mercifully known as just Habs—a school where attendees are required to be wealthy and/or smart, in that order, where the best and brightest "will be challenged by an exciting academic curriculum allied to a wealth of sporting, dramatic, musical and cultural activity." Which sounds a bit like an educational version of Club Med, minus the bikini babes.

Although not a boarding school, Habs maintains an equally strict code of conduct that reflects its mandate to create sophisticated gentleman scholars and discourage rakishness, boorishness, and simple bad form. The rules include:

> *The roof of any building, the woods and water gardens are out of bounds.*

> *Boys are forbidden to possess or use tobacco or alcohol. In the case of senior pupils alcohol may be consumed in moderation with parental permission and under staff supervision on appropriate school occasions specially announced in advance.*

> *Bullying in any form is not tolerated.*

> *Boys are expected to be committed both to their academic work and to the extra-curricular activities of the school. They have an obligation, if selected by the school, to take part in school games and other out-of-school activities and to attend practices and meetings on schooldays, weekends and before term unless special exemption has been granted.*

> *Any action which might bring the school's good name into disrepute, such as contributing to a scurrilous website, is forbidden.*

*All boys are expected to take a pride in their
appearance and to be smartly dressed.*

To attend such a school is to have what's *proper* and *appropriate* drummed into your psyche on a daily basis. But
the curriculum also encouraged freethinking and pushing
the creative envelope. Interestingly, both perspectives can
be seen in Baron Cohen's comedy: If you're going to be inappropriate, at least be entertaining and have a point to it.

One of Sacha's classmates at Habs was Dan Mazer, who
years later would become one of his collaborators. Mazer
and Baron Cohen were the same age, but Sacha was a grade
ahead. Dan recalls the school as being a kind of scholastic
comedy factory, "just cocky young Jews. And because we
were all too weak to fight each other, we compensated
with verbal jousts."

No gangstas in *this* house . . . tuition and costs at Habs
exceed £10,000 a year. *Courtesy of the Haberdashers'
Aske's Boys' School (www.habsboys.org.uk)*

Some remember Sacha standing out for being slightly eccentric. "He seemed to have a basketball permanently attached to his right hand," recalls another former classmate, "which was funny in a school without a basketball team."

Although the Baron Cohens expected their sons to do well academically, the arts were also stressed. The newspaper *The Observer,* which described Daniella as a "forceful Jewish mother," reported that she would urge her sons to perform recitals after the family's Friday-evening Shabbat meals.

Sacha's older brother Erran recalls, "Even in the early days he was the comic and I was the musician."

And then there was that break-dancing phase . . . "As a kid, I was very into rap," Baron Cohen says. When he was twelve, Sacha's mom would load up the linoleum flooring in the back of her Volvo and "take me and my crew . . . to Covent Garden in the dead middle of winter. We'd pull out the lino and start breaking."

At first, the group didn't have an official name. Then, once they started appearing at local bar mitzvahs, Sacha says they called themselves Black On White, and that they "used mainly robotics."

Sacha even provided the entertainment at his own bar mitzvah. "Yes . . . I put down the linoleum on the floor of the Marquis," and with Erran providing the musical background, "me and my crew performed for about an hour and a half."

Sacha's embrace of hip-hop culture didn't go unnoticed. One of his Habs classmates was William Sutcliffe, the novelist. In his first book, *New Boy,* set in a public school not unlike Habs, he described a classmate as a Jewish boy "with floor polish in [his] hair pretending to be [a] ghetto black kid."

Baron Cohen doesn't hedge the characterization. "Essentially we were middle-class Jewish boys who were adopting this culture, which we thought was very cool. That was sort of the origins of Ali G," including the accent, which he and his brother would use while out together.

"I always enjoyed speaking in stupid voices," Sacha says. "I never really spoke as Borat or Bruno, but yeah, I loved playing characters." He also loved watching characters and became a fan of Peter Sellers after seeing a Pink Panther movie when he was eight.

But not everyone found his rap shtick a knee-slapper.

"I always thought Sacha was incredibly full of himself—I never liked him," a former classmate told the *Daily Mail* anonymously. "He was a nice Jewish boy, close to his family, very ambitious, and, to be fair, very talented . . . just incredibly aware of how funny and clever he was, and never modest about it."

Claws bared, the classmate added, "I don't remember Sacha having girlfriends. He wasn't the most attractive of boys so I'm not sure he was a big hitter with the girls. Also, he was quite religious and it wouldn't have been the done thing for him to have lots of girlfriends."

Baron Cohen himself confirms that, as a teenager, he was certainly no ladies' man. "I'm afraid I was never invited to the 'black gates' area," he says, referring to the secluded Habs location where the prep boys would take girls to "cop off."

The perception that it was Judaism that hindered Sacha's romantic development—and not the fact that he attended an all-boys school—is a curious, and perhaps subtly telling, assumption.

Even if he wasn't as devoutly religious as others thought, Sacha was eager to learn about his Jewish culture and was deeply involved with Habonim Dror, a Jewish youth group with chapters in over twenty countries, extending from Zimbabwe to Argentina. The British chapter's Web site states its mission is to "build a Socialist, culturally Jewish future in the state of Israel." Practically speaking, to that end it provides Jewish education, stresses social responsibility, and sponsors summer youth camps.

Sacha, who worked as a *madrich,* or youth leader, downplays any political or social relevance by joking that belonging to Habonim "basically meant that we shared our sweets." But it's clear it provided an outlet for performing. He made his acting debut in a Habonim production of Neil Simon's *Biloxi Blues* and honed his comedy stylings in sketch shows the group put on.

"He was always doing characters, always performing," says a fellow member.

Another recalls the time Baron Cohen did his side-splitting bit about a break-dancing rabbi. (Again, you clearly had to be there.) "I think all of us ten-year-olds hero-worshipped him. He had this ability to capture a roomful of people with his wit and charm and just make us all laugh. When I first saw Ali G I knew straightaway it was our Sacha." He also calls Sacha a good person and with a great artistic presence. "He has been making the Jewish community laugh for years. Now he's making the whole country laugh."

Although "madcap" isn't usually the first thought "Jewish Zionist group" brings to mind, a spokeswoman for his former London Habonim told the *Daily Mail* newspaper, "We think Habonim is where he got his craziness; the confidence in speaking out, feeling comfortable in a crowd—that is what Habonim would have given Sacha."

The ultimate goal of Habonim isn't a life on the boards; it is aliyah, permanent relocation to Israel, but most of the youth opt for an extended stay on a kibbutz instead. So after leaving Habs, Baron Cohen took a one-year sabbatical to Israel, living on the Rosh HaNikra kibbutz, by the sea near the Lebanon border. Established in 1949 by Holocaust survivors and members of the pre-state militia, the kibbutz has around six hundred residents.

Baron Cohen's kibbutz roommate, Elliot Reuben, says that when his work picking avocados was done, Sacha busied himself making short films. "In one, he climbed into a hoist and pretended to be the Messiah ascending to

Sacha slayed them in Rosh HaNikra.

Heaven. In another, he acted out a Western, rolling around in the sand dunes nearby. He was the funniest man in the place by a mile." Of course, there weren't many other people *within* a mile of the isolated kibbutz.

Despite the encouragement, Sacha was reluctant to acknowledge his desire to pursue performing as a career. "I think I was embarrassed to admit to my friends, or myself, that I wanted to be a comic. It was sort of like admitting you wanted to be a model."

So when the year was up, he headed back to England and Cambridge, where it was expected he would study history at the University's Christ's College and follow a long line of Baron Cohens into a proper and appropriate business career.

It didn't quite work out that way.

# 2

# Two-Headed Tradition

IN the **1990s**, Sacha **was** involved **in** the **ARA** (Anti-Racist **Alliance**), **PARTICIPATING** in **MARCHES** against **RACISM** **and** APARTHEID.

**CAMBRIDGE** University is an imposing place. First off, there's its history—having been around since the early thirteenth century, it's one of the oldest learning institutions on the planet. Then there's its size. The university is made up of thirty-one individual, independent colleges. (Think of the university as the U.S. federal government and the colleges as states.) Finally, there's its reputation. In 2006 it was ranked second-highest educational institution in the world, behind only Harvard.

At first glance, Cambridge may seem a place where a break-dancing Jewish boy with an offbeat sense of humor would flounder. But for all its academic reverence, Cambridge is a place that also celebrates the unconventional, appreciating that personal eccentricity can be a by-product of individual genius. That's why the alumni list ranges from John Milton and Charles Darwin to *House*'s Hugh Laurie and Monty Python's John Cleese.

British comic Rowan Atkinson, best known as taciturn

Mr. Bean, notes that it's no coincidence that of the "Monty Python crowd, half of them came from Cambridge, and half of them came from Oxford. . . . There seems to be this jewel, this sort of two-headed tradition of doing comedy, of doing sketches, and that kind of thing," at Britain's most prestigious universities.

Sacha had been accepted at Cambridge's Christ's College to study history. Christ's was founded in 1448 by Henry VI. After the Reformation, it became staunchly puritanical for a while, but Anglican fundamentalism eventually gave way to a more secular, science-based environment courtesy of Victorian England. By the time Sacha landed in Cambridge, the misty, slo-mo *Chariots of Fire* gentility of the early twentieth century had been elbowed aside by edgy Gen X ambition.

Baron Cohen attended Christ's from 1990 to 1993 and managed to maintain a solid grade point average while delving into performing. He joined the Cambridge University Amateur Dramatic Club, better known as simply the ADC. The club has been around since the 1850s and puts on upwards of twenty shows a year. However, depending on one's point of view, the ADC is either steeped in classic drama . . . or a bit stuffy.

The avant garde performing society at Cambridge is Footlights, a comedy troupe that has spawned some of Britain's most successful and popular performers, such as Emma Thompson and most of the Monty Python lads.

Although Baron Cohen participated in the annual Foot-

Sacha was known more for his musical comedy flair than comedy. Could *Ali G: The Musical* be next?
© *Andrew Dunn*

lights review—an evening of sketches and experimental theater—he was never a full-time member and, surprisingly, was more noted for his musical roles than comic prowess. He is credited for saving the day during a university production of *My Fair Lady*.

"We were all terribly worried about it," recalls one of the actors. "It was looking awful, the set wasn't ready on time, and we had all kinds of problems. But on opening night Sacha saved the show by being absolutely brilliant. He had the audience eating out of his hand . . . and in raptures in the big numbers, like 'I'm Getting Married in the Morning.' He obviously had the knack even then."

He also earned glowing reviews as Tevye in *Fiddler on the Roof*. "Sacha sticks in my mind because of that performance," raves Footlights' archivist Dr. Harvey Porter. "I thought he was better than Topol in the West End version—he was marvelous."

In November 1992, Baron Cohen starred in *Cyrano de Bergerac*. The show was produced by Thomas Page, who says he had only a £1,500 budget for the costume drama and five weeks to put it together for its five-day run at the ADC Theatre.

"After several hiccups and pleadings to the ADC Committee for more money, the production went ahead with a cast of forty actors, period costumes for all, an expensive set, a purpose-made latex nose for Cyrano, and a few very expensive classes from a professional sword fight arranger!

"As it turned out, the team selected was one of the most accomplished and professional I worked with at Cambridge," Page says. "The acting was good and the death scene, despite being hammed up, did bring tears to the eyes of more than a few in the audience."

Christ's College head porter,* Jeremy Taylor, says, "I remember Sacha extremely well. He was very outgoing and quite heavily involved in amateur dramatics." Taylor claims he knew Sacha was special all along. "Occasionally you get a student and you think he or she is outstanding. Sacha Baron Cohen stood out as someone who would succeed—so intelligent, but surprisingly quiet. Students come from a variety of backgrounds and leave well-rounded and responsible. Having a part in that is so satisfying."

Others felt Baron Cohen wasn't in his element. "He was a decent enough actor. I recall him doing very well in *Cyrano de Bergerac*," says one acquaintance. "But he was never exactly a leading light."

---

*At Cambridge, a porter is a kind of university jack-of-all-trades. Their duties can include security work, sorting mail, and maintenance. Think concierge for privileged students.

Sacha says his experience and the acting skills he honed in the ADC would prove particularly useful later on "to create comic characters that were believable and real and weren't larger than life."

And his musical and dramatic kudos notwithstanding, characters were what Sasha wanted to do. "I started developing characters partly as a way to get into places without paying," he says. "At Cambridge there was something called the Cambridge balls, which at that time cost about one hundred and twenty pounds per head. I would try to get myself and other people in pretending to be the band or something." Sacha admits that several years later, while in New York, he and his friends would gain admittance to clubs "claiming we were bouncers or drug dealers."

His wild and crazy Habonim superiors would have been so proud.

But when not onstage or in character, Sacha—who then was skinny and sported horn-rimmed glasses— tended to be quiet and reserved. He still is. "If you sat next to him at dinner," a friend once noted, "you might come away thinking how sweet and clever he is, and so very funny . . . for an accountant."

To his academic instructors, Baron Cohen was a serious, socially proactive intellectual who was particularly interested in studying the roots of ethnic and cultural prejudices. He spent a summer in America researching his dissertation on the role played by Jews in the civil-rights movement. Titled "The Black/Jewish Allies: A Case of

Mistaking Identity," the paper focused on the 1964 murders of three young civil-rights workers in Philadelphia, Mississippi, at the hands of the local Ku Klux Klan. James Chaney, who was black, lived in Mississippi; Andrew Goodman and Michael Schwerner were northern Jews who had gone South to help register black voters.

"I was writing this at the time of the Crown Heights riots when the Jewish community was obsessed with black anti-Semitism," he recalls. His thematic argument was that this obsession was born out of deep feelings of betrayal because many Jews saw themselves as an integral part of the civil-rights movement and considered black Americans "their old blood brothers. . . . But while it was perceived in the Jewish community that Jews were disproportionately involved in civil rights, my conclusion was black Americans didn't see Jews as being more involved than any white Americans."

The disconnect came because even though there were a significant number of Jewish youths working in the South, "because they were there as part of church organizations like the [Southern Christian Leadership Council], they weren't seen as Jews but as white liberals. So there was this deep irony that the Jewish establishment took martyrs like Andrew Goodman and Michael Schwerner and used them as symbols of a Jewish/black alliance when, in fact, they didn't really see themselves as Jews at all."

As if concerned that he is perhaps revealing too much of himself, Baron Cohen falls back on humor and dryly notes, "The dissertation is a lot funnier than I depicted it."

Sacha's history instructor Dr. Tony Badger said the dissertation was "outstanding," in part because Baron Cohen managed to score an interview with Robert Moses, a Harlem-born, Harvard-educated math teacher who became an influential civil-rights advocate in 1960s Mississippi, stressing the importance of education in the fight for racial and economic equality.

"Moses was revered, deified by some, and he was not talking to anybody," says Cambridge school chum Clive Webb. "To this day I have no idea how Sacha managed to pull it off."

"Bob Moses never does interviews," concurs Dr. Badger. "But Sacha was in Boston and looked him up in the phone directory, met him for breakfast, and got him to do one—perhaps a foretelling of things to come."

Sacha's ability to ingratiate himself with people aside, the notion that individual perceptions and expectations are largely born from our cultural viewpoints—and often become the basis for ethnic and religious distrust and misunderstanding—inspired him as a potentially rich and daring comic mine to plumb. One unlikely source of inspiration was Third Reich historian Ian Kershaw, who wrote: "The path to Auschwitz was paved with indifference." Cohen notes, "I know it's not very funny being a comedian talking about the Holocaust, but I think it's an interesting idea that not everyone in Germany had to be a raving anti-Semite. They just had to be apathetic."

Baron Cohen wanted to ruffle feathers, for both comic

effect and to expose subconscious biases carefully buried under political correctness or ignored out of apathy. But the line between satire and boorishness is a thin one, and occasionally blurs. The trick was finding the right format.

That Sacha would attempt to blend his social awareness with his zeal for performing was no surprise to Dan Mazer, who had attended Habs with Baron Cohen but didn't become friends with him until they ended up at Cambridge together.

"He was a cultural polyglot,* and that's the nature of Cambridge," Mazer explains. "Your interests become quite eclectic."

Naturally, Baron Cohen's parents had hoped their son would pursue a career in business or perhaps even in academia, like his noted cousin Simon Baron-Cohen. Professor Baron-Cohen is a professor of developmental psychopathology at, of all places, Cambridge. (A coincidence? We think not. . . .)

Simon and a team of colleagues made headlines with their research that indicated characteristics deemed socially as "male" (analytical skills and mathematical aptitude) and "female" (compassion, emotionalism) are determined biochemically in the womb prior to birth, meaning that we are less influenced—or changed—by our environment than we like to think. It's the kind of finding that adds weight to Sacha's premise that bias and

---

*Polyglot: someone who is multilingual. "Cultural polyglot" is Cambridge-speak for "well rounded."

prejudice may be more ingrained than is comfortable to contemplate.

Sacha graduated from Cambridge with a 2:1 honors (Upper Second Class) in his history degree.* From the "is nothing ever good enough for you?" file, Dr. Badger expresses the opinion that it was Baron Cohen's extracurricular performance activities that kept him from reaching his full academic potential and earning a 1:1.

University degree safely in hand, Baron Cohen now had a choice to make: follow convention or follow his passion? He compromised by limiting his window of opportunity, giving himself a five-year window to start earning enough money as an actor or a performer to support himself. "If it didn't work out, I was going to move on to something else, become a barrister or something."

With the clock ticking, Sacha set out to forge a comic identity. In the process, he would come up with several.

---

*Instead of using an A–F grading scale, Cambridge uses a 1–9 system, with 1 being the highest. Sacha graduated with upper second class honors.

# 3

# A Clown Is Born

LET'S talk ABOUT when TECHNOLOGY goes horribly wrong: Could THERE be ANOTHER Nintendo 64? —Ali G

**COLLEGE** has a way of preparing students academically for the real world while frequently leaving them to flap emotionally and practically in the wind. The deal is supposed to be: work hard to graduate and in turn get rewarded for your determination and talent with the career of your choice. The only problem is, the rest of the world seldom gets the memo.

Even though he gave himself a five-year cushion, Sacha expected big things as soon as he left Cambridge. "I did a very pretentious play which won an award. I thought: *I'm going to be huge*—and then spent the next two years sweeping the floor in a restaurant."

Picking up the withered pieces of his popped expectations, Sacha hit the pavement like every other struggling actor. In April 1995 Baron Cohen made his television debut in the Channel 4 comedy *Jack and Jeremy's Police 4*. The half-hour special was a takeoff on *Crimewatch*, Britain's version of *America's Most Wanted*, with popular comedians

The anti–Ali G

Jack Dee and Jeremy Hardy playing low-level police officers. Viewers were invited to vote on whether one of the criminals should be *spared* or *chaired*. Of the 250,000 who phoned in, 3 voted for mercy; the rest clamored for a fry-fest.

That same year Sacha was hired as a presenter for a show called *Pump TV,* broadcast from a small satellite station in Slough, a town on the outskirts of London near Heathrow Airport. In pictures from that time Baron Cohen exudes an unnatural perkiness, with a big-collared shirt and plastered-down hair, a kind of pre–George Clooney "Caesar" look.

Sacha conducted interviews with local "personalities," such as a young girl in a cat costume and a calligraphy instructor. Although Baron Cohen played these interviews straight, hints of his sardonic humor peeked through. When a band called Happy Pills performed, he introduced them as "the angry sound of Slough youth."

Nor could Sacha hide his intellect. "We looked down on him because he was working on a crap local TV show," lead singer Lewis Batt told the *Daily Mail*. "[But] I remember him using the phrase 'interesting philosophical

Sacha interviewing a
local personality

conundrum.' . . ."

Leander Morales from the group GM3 remembers Sacha as being "very funny, but there was a definite sarcastic edge. . . . We were stuck in a studio about twenty-five feet by thirty feet and the number of people watching was so small that when they had a phone-in, staff in the next-door office would have to ring in to keep the show going."

While *Pump TV* may not have been great art, it was a great training ground. "The budget was about forty pounds a week, and we had a viewership of about fifty to sixty people," Baron Cohen says. "But it gave me access to a crew and an editing room, so we started experimenting with making these little short films, which generally never got broadcast."

The operative word being "generally."

"One time, on Valentine's night, two of the guys who were working with me broke into the studio and transmitted all the sketches that never made it to air. They got fired."

Alas, not long after, the channel succumbed to fatal ratings and Baron Cohen was back among the unemployed-actor

ranks. For a while he shared an apartment with his older
brother Erran. An aspiring composer and musician, Erran
understood Sacha's drive. "Music has been my life," Erran
says. "I'd rather just play at weddings and bar mitzvahs than
do any other job."

The brothers' shared passion for performing forged a
deep bond between them. "We have supported and criticized each other through our careers," Erran says. He recalls the time in 1996 when he needed some Spanish
dialogue for a recording he was making. "Sacha came up
with the goods just like that and rattled off a Spanish gib-
berish riddle he somehow knew. It sounded fantastic on
the track—he has always been good with accents and that
is why he is such a good comedian."

One of the first times Erran teamed up with his brother
professionally onstage was for a comedy sketch in a West
Hampstead club. "It was Sacha's idea for the sketch called
'Shvitzing'—the Yiddish word for 'sweating.'"

The premise was about two Hassidic Jews who became
overheated in their heavy clothing, so they stripped down
to their Orthodox skivvies. Erran accompanied the skit on
the piano.

They performed "Shvitzing" and got an enthusiastic reception. Buoyed, Sacha decided to pitch it for television.
First, they took it to BBC Two, which regularly featured
short films in between its regular programming and as a
channel was considered . . . how to say this nicely . . . a
bit *lowbrow*.

BBC Two passed on "Shvitzing," thinking it was in bad taste.

Undaunted, the brothers then went to BBC, the high-brow mother ship of British public television. The Beeb declined, calling the skit offensive.

It was obvious these characters were DOA to television executives, so Sacha chucked the Hassids and started over. It was time to get serious and start clowning around. We're talking Clown with a capital *C*. Although many people dismiss clowning as little more than shtick with a water-squirting flower and face paint, the *art* of clowning has a long, revered history in dramatic circles.

After graduating from Cambridge, Baron Cohen spent a year studying with drama teacher Philippe Gaulier, who is considered a master at clowning and *bouffon*.*

"The clown character allows you to show your greatest strength," Gaulier says. "Most people are nice. Or small. Or self-constrained. They're so *boooorrriinng* that nobody sees them.

"But being boring is normal. Sometimes you have to be boring before you can discover something new. That's when the craft of theater is so useful. We can learn to become larger characters by becoming more like our true selves."

Considering some of Sasha's later gags with Ali G and Borat, that's a deeply ~~disturbing~~ interesting concept.

---

*Clowning is performance that acknowledges the audience and includes physical comedy. *Bouffon* is a darker form of clowning. Think the evil twin.

Gaulier's purpose is to help people find their inner clown, a process one of his students describes as "open-heart surgery without anesthetic."

And to think, people actually pay for the privilege. . . .

For Baron Cohen, it was money—and pain—well spent. "During the time I studied with him he was brutally honest, constantly reminding me of when my performance was rubbish and very occasionally telling me when it was not so bad. Gaulier was so lacking in pretension that he made acting what it should be, which is *fun*. Without him, I really do doubt whether I would have had any success in my field."

Gaulier acknowledges Sacha's talent, "He was a good clown, full of spirit," but swats away the compliment as if it's a pesky fly. "I don't feel any responsibility for [my students'] success. . . . I don't teach a special style; what I teach more is a wonderful spirit," he explains. "People have to find a way of being beautiful and surprising."

Sacha's next job was for the satellite channel Talk TV. Talk TV was owned by Granada Sky Broadcasting, a joint venture between Granada and Sky that, due to poor viewing figures, ceased broadcasting in 1997. On the Talk TV channel there was an afternoon kids' talk show called *F2F*. In 1997, Sasha was hired to be an *F2F*[*] presenter.

---

[*]A must-have for the ultimate SBC fan: You can license your very own video clips from the *F2F* pilot featuring Sacha at www.itnsource.com.

The show's director, Mike Toppin, became a mentor of sorts to Sacha. Toppin urged the young comic to expand his characters and imbue them with more of a distinct voice. Finally, Baron Cohen had the platform he needed to more effectively incorporate Gaulier's training.

"The idea was that I would host the show and then we would play some prerecorded segments of me appearing as these different characters, who would comment on myself as a host," Sacha explains.

One of those characters is an early version of Ali G. Baron Cohen readily admits he was inspired by BBC radio personality Tim Westwood. Although white as an English Easter lily, Westwood was—and still is—a self-styled hip-hop DJ who embraced a romanticized image of the urban gangsta.

Easy to posture when you've never actually been to South Central L.A.

This Eminem wannabe is the middle-class son of a preacher who attended public school on the not-so-mean streets of Lowestoft, Suffolk. (It's telling that on its police

Tim Westwood, gangsta . . . not!

department Web site all of the officers pictured are white.) After becoming a DJ and making rap his genre of choice, Westwood traded his Suffolk accent for a generic faux Caribbean dialect.

Matthew Bannister, who worked with Westwood at Radio 1, told the *Daily Mail* that "the first thing you're always conscious of with Tim is the Puffa jacket. It comes through the door first, then the boots and then the trousers, which are twenty times too big with the crotch hanging down."

Hmm . . . sound familiar?

The fact is, for a comic you simply cannot make this stuff up. But you can sure use it.

Being a longtime fan of rap himself, Baron Cohen listened to Westwood on the radio; like many others, he had thought that the DJ was black, "because he sounded like a New York gangsta," when in fact he was a "tall, skinny white guy.

"We used to go to these hip-hop happenings, and even then he was kind of laughable. Once I found out that he was actually the son of a bishop, it became even more absurd. He was so keen to be presented as a gangsta."

Sacha found the entire wannabe mentality of middle-class whites pretending to be black equally fascinating. "The ones who ring Tim Westwood's rap show on behalf of the 'Liverpool Sainsbury's Massive,'* the ones who act like they're in South Central L.A. and talk about motherfuckers."

---

*In case you don't know, Massive is slang for a localized gang.

The first prototype of what would eventually morph into Ali G was called MC Jocelyn Cheadle-Hume, whom Sacha describes as "a hip-hop journalist, a wankster reporter." One day when Sacha and Mike were out filming a segment, they ran into a group of young skateboarders. Sacha says Toppin "gave me a little nod and I approached them and started interacting with them in character." To Sacha's amazement, the youths assumed he was legit. When he showed off his artless skateboarding moves, "they were laughing and mocking me. After a couple of minutes, I went back to my normal voice and said, 'You know, this is a character.' And they were really surprised. At which point I realized that people *would* believe me when I did this character."

It was an adrenaline-fueled *eureka!* moment. So when a tour bus happened to stop nearby, Sacha jumped on with his camera and went back into character. "I took the microphone and I was like, 'Yo, check it out. I is here, and this is me bus.' Booyakasha."

He recalls the experience in mental snapshots: commandeering the tourist bus, entering a pub, break dancing for the surprised patrons, marching into the offices of the multinational company where his father worked and where, "essentially, we were thrown out by security after about twenty minutes." But no matter. The real realization was: "There was never a question of whether I was really this character or not."

Later, as he and Toppin were walking back to the London

Weekend Television studio, Baron Cohen remembers crossing over the Waterloo Bridge with their adrenaline still
pumping. "We were just so excited, because here was this
new form of comedy. . . . Probably it existed and other people had done it, but *we'd* never discovered it before—this
idea of taking a comic character into a real situation."

Still punch-drunk, they couldn't wait to broadcast the
segments they had filmed. Before the second clip had even
finished, the head of the channel called to demand they
take it off the air. Immediately.

Sacha recalls the executive sputtering, "'What do you
think you're doing? We're gonna get sued!' It was at that
point that I knew that we were doing something that might
be good."

Now that he had gotten a taste of how he could
creatively use characters, he started trying out some
others—such as a loudly dressed Moldavian reporter
named Alexi Krickler who was unrelentingly confused by
British culture and traditions. The inspiration for Alexi
came from a doctor that Sacha had met several years earlier
while vacationing in Astrakhan, Russia, with a friend. He
found the doctor's accent and cultural observations inex-
plicably hilarious. "You are from England. You say 'cock,'
Americans say 'cahk.'"

"This guy got me and my friend crying with laughter. I
really didn't know why it was. He had some elements of
Borat, but he had none of the racism or the misogyny or

the anti-Semitism. He was Jewish, actually."

Flash forward to Sacha's comic epiphany after that day on the bus. "When I started developing this whole undercover comedy, I knew I wanted to develop a foreign character and I was in my car and I had the cameraman in the back and I said, 'All right, let's get out here.' And he said, 'Where's the character going to be from?'"

While thinking, Sacha happened to glance in the back of the car and spotted a hat from Astrakhan—an heirloom from his vacation in Russia. He put the hat on and decided to make the character Moldavian. And it was in this seemingly simple way that the original, early form of Borat was born. Sacha roamed the streets in the East End of London asking unsuspecting pedestrians to explain questions such as, "What is it to be a cocksman?" Which they did in thoughtful detail. "I just felt here's this really brilliant mechanism that was naive and simple and childlike and warm and loveable . . . but this real tool to get people to expose themselves."

Perhaps the most surprising thing was how tolerant the average aristocrat on the street was. "I was struck by the patience of some of these members of the upper class, who were so keen to appear polite—particularly on camera—that they would never walk away."

His other incarnation was a flamboyant, celebrity-struck fashion reporter named Bruno, who regularly forgets his questions once the interview starts. Sacha debuted Bruno in a short segment aired on the Paramount Comedy Channel during London's Fashion Week in 1998.

Despite the accumulating television airtime, Baron Cohen was still not making a sustainable living at performing. *Rolling Stone* reported that "he was so broke he often had to wear Ali G's clothes when he went out." (Dad couldn't float him an outfit or two from one of the family stores?)

Wardrobe, though, was not his problem—time was. His self-imposed deadline was just two months away. For all he had accomplished, there was no guarantee he wouldn't remain a small-time bit player. He remembers sitting on a beach in Thailand after having attended his brother's wedding in Australia, and contemplating just staying there. "I was having this very nice life on a pound-fifty a day. And that's when I got a call from my agent saying there's this audition for *The 11 O'Clock Show*." The late-night comedy show was seeking a new host. Although it sounded like a perfect fit for Sacha, "I remember telling her that I didn't know if I wanted to come back. I had been rejected so many times that I didn't know if it was worth it."

Once he stopped feeling sorry for himself, Baron Cohen had his agent arrange an interview. Initially the producers were underwhelmed with Sacha—until they saw a video of Alexi interviewing some attendees at a pro–fox hunt rally in Hyde Park. At one point, Alexi asked some hunters if England could relieve prison overcrowding by releasing inmates instead of foxes and letting *them* be chased by the hounds.

"Bloody good idea," one agreed.

Sacha was hired and life as he knew it was about to change forever.

# 4

# The Gangsta from Staines

DA *ALI G SHOW* prompted **SENSITIVITY** training for **U.K.** police **ON CULTURAL** stereotyping.

**THE** *11 O'Clock Show* was a uniquely British comedy confection that embraced satire and vulgarity with equal gusto. (It spawned the likes of *The Daily Show* and *Jackass* in the US.)

Ongoing tinkering gave the show, touted as a sketch comedy, a work-in-progress kinetic energy. Regular bits included tongue-in-cheek commentary on the day's news, man-in-the-street commentary, and in-studio interviews. The show aired three times a week, with a best-of compilation show broadcast on the weekend.

Because actual news headlines were used as fodder, *The 11 O'Clock Show* filmed the same day it aired, making for harried deadlines and hit-or-miss writing—that live TV syndrome where, while a majority of bits fell short, there were enough laughs to keep the core audience tuning back in.

The program was the brainchild of the late Harry

In 2005, a few hours after marrying longtime girlfriend Lisa Whadcock, Harry Thompson died from inoperable lung cancer. He was forty-five. *British Broadcasting Corporation*

Thompson, widely considered one of the most important comedy producers in British television history. One BBC executive described Thompson as "that rarity in television—the talented, single-minded, subversive maverick."

A Renaissance man, Thompson was also an acclaimed journalist, nonfiction author, and novelist.

Actor Paul Whitehouse remembers Thompson as someone who had a very specific comic vision. "If he thought something was a pile of shit, he'd tell us. . . . He helped with the how and where you get to a punch line."

Thompson saw himself as a kind of humor negotiator. "As a producer, you decide what goes in the show and what doesn't. You stand or fall by that. So I find myself arguing over jokes a lot. You end up being a bit of a Liberal Democrat, trying to rein people into the center."

He was particularly skillful at recognizing comedic potential and finding the right vehicle to showcase that talent. The story goes that after hiring Sacha, "Thompson sat him down one day and told him to forget about the other characters he was working up in order to concentrate on a

Staines's statue
of lino workers

spoof *yoof*\* commentator. "That afternoon," says White-house, "the immortal Ali G was born."

Thompson described the character, with his designer duds and bling, as "the disaffected wannabe homeboy of the suburbs, the kid stuck in Staines† who dreamed of Compton or Watts." Thompson suggested the name Ali G because "we thought, if he had a whiff of Islam about him, people would be afraid to challenge him," out of political correctness.

But Baron Cohen intentionally made Ali G ethnically vague, believing ambiguity was vital for the character's persona. "The important thing about Ali G is that he's not black . . . and he is delusional," explains Baron Cohen, "so

---

\*A phrase originally coined by Janet Street-Porter as head of the BBCs youth and entertainment features.

†Staines is the former linoleum manufacturing capital of the world. The factory closed in 1970, but a bronze statue of two "lino" workers remains.

he believes he is a black hip-hop artist from Staines. He believes his neighborhood is a rough ghetto when in fact it's this lovely, leafy, middle-class suburb outside Windsor where swans swim under the beautiful bridge." Sacha stresses that focusing on his ethnicity is missing the point. "It's important that he's deluded."

According to his imaginatively constructed backstory, Ali G moved in with his grandmother to care for her after his parents died. Of course, Ali G tells his tale much more colorfully. (To the untrained ear his faux gansta accent can be hard to decipher at first . . . bear with me while I try to do it justice in the written word.) "Me woz failed by da skool system and hated every minute me spent in da classroom. In fact, added together, dat time woz probly da most borin' three hours of me life. Altho me do still go to a skool re-union every second Monday at Staines Job Center."

The first series* of *The 11 O'Clock Show* debuted on September 30, 1998, and ran a week. The basic format had two hosts and a merry band of correspondents; everyone but Baron Cohen interviewed people as themselves. The reception was positive enough that Channel 4 ordered a second series, which began on March 9, 1999 and ran eight weeks. Season three followed in October.

---

*Between October 1998 and December 2000 *The 11 O'Clock Show* is listed as having had five series, but only credited with having three good ones. . . .

Ali G was presented as the "voice of disaffected youth" and almost instantly became the focus of viewers' attentions. The conceit of the character was Sacha's ploy of playing Ali G's outlandishness straight so that those he interviewed would really think he was a sincere, albeit intellectually challenged, representative of his peers.

According to a profile in the *Living Scotsman* newspaper, "The interviewees were told beforehand they were participating in an educational programme aimed at getting young people interested in important issues. In order to get the issues over, the interviewer was a young person who did not understand the issues himself."

And as Thompson correctly predicted, political correctness prevented the majority of people from telling Ali G to get a brain and fuck off. Elected officials, politicians, social leaders, and other members of the British establishment, apparently hoping to either curry favor with or prove they were still in touch with the country's youth, displayed superhuman patience—and often surprising insight—as Ali G's idiocy lowered their defenses.

When conservative politician Sir Teddy Taylor was asked if Jamaica being excluded from the European Community was *racialist,* he later shrugged off the malapropism. "As a long-standing Bob Marley fan—who often plays his songs on the road from the Commons to Southend—I felt quite at home with Ali's West Indian accent."

One of Ali G's early interviews was with ultraliberal former member of Parliament Tony Benn. "At no stage during our talk did I suspect that it was anything other than a genuine program," says Taylor. "Ali G was courteous and friendly . . . and, in his first question, he asked me to explain socialism. He seemed to believe it was the same as the welfare state."

At one point Ali G suggested workers went on strike "just coz they is lazy and want to chill for a day or so."

As it was still early in the interview, Benn says he decided "the only respectful thing to do was to argue with him and to do so as vigorously as I could."

You say *vigorously;* I say *outraged.*

At one point Benn told Ali: "You've got no time for people, you think they're lazy, greedy, don't want to work, you call women bitches, and then you're asking me about a society that's happy."

The politician later told *Radio Times:* "Even after I left the studio I thought it was genuine . . . although I was a bit suspicious when he said Margaret Thatcher was a communist."

When the interview was broadcast, Benn admits, "I was furious when I first discovered what was really going on and even wrote to Channel 4 to protest. . . . But there was a sequel which showed it all in a different light."

More appeasing than that was the reaction from the public. Benn admits that many of his younger constituents approached him on the street, or wrote in, "to say how much they had enjoyed it and how glad they were that I had stood up to him. Now that I know how the comedian works, I've become a big fan of his work. The programs were what

Channel 4 had said they would be—a chance to present politics to young people. Ali G is a clever man, and I am beginning to wonder if that was what he actually intended to do."

Sacha indicates it indeed was. While he allows that certain participants, like Tony Benn, were initially upset at the tactics, they realized afterward that "it was actually beneficial for their careers or their status. . . . Because he had this ignoramus in the room with him, who was espousing the most right-wing and totally selfish attitudes, he was able to put down Ali G and put his own viewpoint across."

The late Professor Sue Lees, a leading British feminist, recalled her encounter with Ali G in a 2000 *Sunday Mail* interview:

> I was worried my reputation would be in tatters but I felt much better when he confused feminism with lesbianism, saying: "I know girls who have tried feminism at parties—then next day they go back to their boyfriends."
>
> I suppose what he threw at me were all the popular misconceptions . . . accusing feminists of being lesbians, and berating women for not being able to do the things men could . . . inadvertently allowing me to shatter some of those myths. However, it all became a little surreal when Ali started going into the weird sexual practices of his uncle.
>
> But I can't moan. It's reached an audience

that nothing else I've ever done with television could. And I suppose, in an odd way, it gets the message across. But I'd have much rather been told what I was letting myself in for.

Even the clergy was fair game. After Bishop Lindsay Urwin told Ali G he did indeed believe in miracles, he was challenged to make his chair levitate. "At that point, I knew I'd been had. I think the exact words that went through my mind were, *Oh, bloody hell*." The bishop proudly recalls his snappy comeback: "I think it will be more of a miracle if I could find someone who loved you."

While Ali tried the clergyman's patience when he questioned the Virgin Mary—"When I told him I believed in the virgin birth he said: 'But that's what all the girls say'"—in the end, Sacha points out, "it's my character who looks the idiot. The subjects come across as really nice, tolerant people. I liked the Bishop of Horsham so much I stuck around for half an hour trying to persuade him to give up his vow of celibacy."

Urwin, who was only forty-two at the time of the interview, recalled to the *Daily Mail*:

> He couldn't get to grips with the idea of my never having sex. When I said there weren't hordes of women trying to dissuade me from my chosen path, he quipped: "I could arrange that for you, Bish."

Now, whenever I visit local secondary schools in Horsham, Sussex, I get the full attention of the kids, who shout things like "nuff respect." So I can forgive Ali for taking me for a ride. It was an interesting one.

Former education secretary Rhodes Boyson also enjoyed his encounter:

> I think I proved a feisty opponent. It started when he walked into my home wearing what looked like a big yellow balloon. It was pure comedy right from the off, anyone who can't see that must be wrong in the head. . . .
>
> But he's an intelligent man. We had what can only be described as a game of mental chess for two hours. I played it for what it was—an enormous exercise in leg-pulling.

Sometimes, even Sacha worried he may have gone too far. After his interview with Ali G, scientist and inventor Heinz Wolff steered him into a small office and pulled out a rifle. "I honestly thought he was going to kill me," Sacha says, "but he just wanted to demonstrate that you can't fire an air gun pellet through cling-film."

But the iconic moment for Ali G came when he was led away from an environmental protest by a policeman and Ali G asked with righteous indignation, "Is it coz I'ze black?"

Without so much as a double take that a white man had asked the question, the cop calmly assured Ali that being black had nothing to do with it. "Is it coz I'ze black?" would become a British pop cultural catchphrase for everything false and pretentious.

Ali G was a bona fide phenomenon and Sacha Baron Cohen was the new comic golden boy—and he no longer worried about making a living. His work on *The 11 O'Clock Show* earned him the 1999 British Comedy Award for Best Male Comedy Newcomer. *Da Best of Ali G*, a compilation of his interviews from *The 11 O'Clock Show*, became a huge seller, as did the *Ali G, Innit* and *Ali G, Aiii* videos.

Exactly why Ali G touched such a chord was the subject of spirited debate. Media pundit Simon Couth suggested:

> There is the allure in demystifying celebrities and taking his B-list subjects down a peg or two. As my students say, "We like it when he puts those snotty types in their place."
>
> And . . . it is a tried and tested TV technique formula. What the TV industry does is to bombard audiences with lots of mediums and sketches and formats. It's safe—and then you pick out things that work.

Couth also considered Ali G's success a product of skilled marketing:

Students don't like hype. The Channel 4 strategy works because it is not over-hyping him. Counterculture is about not making the name too well known and successful—they want to keep him 'our' person and they don't want him in the public domain.

Keeping him under wraps with the audience means he is exclusive to them. If you saw him at every celebrity bash, he becomes like his own targets.

Ali G had become bigger than *The 11 O'Clock Show,* so it was hardly a surprise when it was announced Baron Cohen would get his own series, titled—what else?—*Da Ali G Show*.

While success might not have spoiled Ali G, it did bring subtle changes to the character. Some would see it as growth, while others would see it as self-aggrandizement. And through it all, Sacha Baron Cohen remained his enigmatic self.

# 5

# The Ali G Juggernaut

**DIS** iz **GONNA** be **like** *60 MINUTES*, but **JUS'** wid **more sex.** —ALI G

**FROM** the "it's a small Cambridge alumni world after all" file, the producer for Sasha's show was his old Habs schoolmate Dan Mazer. While the behind-the-scenes image of comedy shows is zaniness and puerile fun, in a 2006 interview with Daniel Robert Epstein, Mazer made his collaboration with Sacha sound about as fun as an Ibsen marathon. When Epstein commented that it must be fun to work together, Mazer shrugged. "Not really," he laughed. "It's true that comedy is a very serious business. It is one of those weird things where it becomes work and your laughs are work related."

Mazer admitted that as a schoolboy Sacha was always the most outgoing, gregarious one in the room. "He was such a big personality that I didn't envision him being able to hide himself so well" behind characters.

Ali G's popularity had blown his anonymity, so by necessity the character needed to be tweaked for the new show. So when the show premiered in March 2000, viewers were introduced to a new Ali G. Instead of relying on the political-based satire of his earlier incarnation, Mazer and Baron Cohen had collaborated to give the former "idiot" a harder edge. Before, Ali had been the butt of the joke; now he set up his subjects to be the punch line.

Not everyone minded. Former MP Neil Hamilton claims he knew immediately what game was afoot and played along. He had watched a tape of Ali G interviewing Tony Benn and found it "hilarious . . . Ali mopped him up. For me, doing the show was just another commercial engagement." Hamilton acknowledges that putting himself in such a position carried some risk. He recalls: "The most startling thing was when Ali offered me what looked like a joint. I took it and went along with the gag, having a few puffs. The audience went wild, so I suppose it had the desired effect, for Ali at least. Not being streetwise about these things, to this day I have no idea if it was really marijuana. I didn't suffer any ill effects."

But some viewers felt the new show did. "On *The 11 O'Clock Show,* he was a stupid, uninformed waster, who wanted to be a black rapper, who thought drugs and violence and rap were cool because his friends told him so," wrote one fan, who called the "all-too-accurate" parody "hilariously funny" because it pricked the bubble of modern-day British youth.

But some of the fun went away for this viewer once Ali G began headlining his own show. Instead of playing the fool, Sacha became the winking master of ceremonies, turning "Ali into a character you laughed with rather than at. He was in on the joke." While still funny, the viewer concluded, it was "no way near as clever."

*Daily Mail*'s Glenda Cooper noted: "As the humor has become blunter, the language has become coarser and the 'gangsta rapper' now seems little different from the figures he is supposedly mocking." Cooper felt Baron Cohen had forfeited his comic edge and pointed out that there was a growing sentiment among some fans that perhaps Ali G's moment was nearing an end.

Cooper questioned whether or not Sacha was squandering his comic potential. Whereas once he was hailed as Britain's answer to Woody Allen, "an acute observer of contemporary Jewish life with wide appeal," Cohen "appears to have been dissuaded from exploring this avenue by his more religious friends, who fear it might be offensive to the Jewish community." Cooper also suggested that criticism of Ali G was increasing because the character had become more style than substance.

The change in tone struck a raw nerve. An article in *The Mirror* commented: "Baron Cohen is a nice Jewish boy from Hampstead who has made millions taking the piss out of black culture. Or does anyone still buy the line that Baron Cohen is actually mocking white boys who want to be black?"

Black British comic Felix Dexter noted, "Baron Cohen allows the liberal middle classes to laugh at black street culture in a context where they can retain their sense of political correctness."

An editorial in *The Guardian* declared: "The fact that he has been a success should not be treated as an excuse to quash discussion about the propriety of the act. If the black and white minstrels weren't funny, then why is Ali G?"

*The Observer*'s Jay Rayner commented:

> Keeping himself and his creation separate makes an awful lot of sense for Baron Cohen. It means he never has to engage with the debate over his act. He never apologizes, never explains. But the early joke was soon blown and over the past few years Ali G has had to be repositioned. If anything, that has made the contradictions more pronounced.
>
> A few years ago, figures in the black community were describing him as a deeply offensive stereotype. Last week, by joining up with [hip-hop artist] Shaggy, Baron Cohen started moving his one bankable product into the heart of that culture. Is he now ridiculing its misogyny and the apparent adoration of gun violence, or is he co-opting it?
>
> Of course, he will not say. He never does. But nothing he is doing is casual.

The rumbling grew loud enough that Channel 4 felt obliged to defend their personality. "He is about a white kid pretending to be black," a spokesman explained. "He is satirizing the way white kids try to copy the black street culture and look ridiculous. If it's offensive to anyone, it's offensive to white people."

Harry Thompson, cocreator and producer of *Da Ali G Show,* maintained it was just comedy as usual. "Ali has become a cultural magnet for inarticulate youth in the 2000s. It's a perverse but welcome accolade for one of the most brilliant comic talents that I've ever encountered."

The criticism prompted Sacha's mother, Daniella, to tell *The Mirror,* "Allegations that he is being racist are rubbish. My son wrote a thesis about Jewish involvement in the black American [civil-rights] movement. Ali G may be anti-establishment, but young people like him because they see themselves in him. I think Ali G is wonderful."

Not everyone agreed. In May 2000 the *Sunday Mail* in Glasgow reported that a neo-Nazi organization called Combat 18 had sent hate letters to Sacha threatening to kill him.

"Police are taking the threats seriously and are to meet Channel 4 bosses to talk about security measures to protect the star." According to the report, the hand-written letters were sent to Channel 4's London office, which in turn forwarded the threats to Talk Back, the production company which makes *Da Ali G Show.* "The company immediately called in Scotland Yard, whose officers had no doubt about the authenticity of the letters."

The irony? Combat 18 is known for targeting high-profile black people.

Hopefully the members of Combat 18 read the paper and finally realized Baron Cohen was not, in fact, black.

But as much as his supporters wanted to portray Sacha as the misunderstood and unfairly maligned artist, it contradicted a very basic fact: Baron Cohen meticulously controlled every aspect of his career.

"The attention to detail is absolutely staggering," says a former coworker.

If there was controversy surrounding Ali G, it was hard not to believe it was because that's exactly what Sacha wanted. And the attention made him one of the most famous men in Britain and the undisputed It boy of the moment. The proof? In the spring of 2000, 36 percent of eleven- to sixteen-year-olds polled wanted Ali G to be elected mayor of London. More proof? Madonna asked Sacha to appear in the music video for her new single, "Music."

Sacha told Howard Stern that when she called he thought it was someone pulling a prank and started goofing on her. It took nearly ten minutes for her to convince him she was really Madonna. The singer's manager, Caresse Norman, says Madonna became a fan after seeing his video *Ali G, Innit*. "Madonna loves him. He is such a doll. She still can't stop laughing. She watched the tape and thought he was brilliant—the Peter Sellers of his generation."

The two became such buds that Baron Cohen invited her to meet his family. Sacha's brother Erran called the night Madonna and her husband, director Guy Ritchie, came to his mother's house for tea "surreal." Referring to Madonna

"I ain't sayin' nothin', but next time you look at little Rocco, imagine him with a goatee beard and yellow glasses, a'ight?"

as the most famous person in the world, Erran says, "It was not what you would call your average family meal. Madonna brought 'round a copy of the final cut of her 'Music' video and we all sat 'round the TV and watched it." After dinner, Erran played chess with Guy Ritchie, supposedly letting Guy win.

Sacha's reaction to fame was to hide ever further behind his on-camera persona. He declined to give any interviews— or make any public appearances—as himself. It was Ali G or nothing. Baron Cohen was so successful at sublimating himself in Ali G that few would recognize him when he stepped out from behind his Hilfiger. But in 2000 fans had a chance to see Baron Cohen in a very different role.

Written and directed by Christopher Payne, *The Jolly Boys' Last Stand* was a coming-of-adult-age story about a group of twentysomething friends faced with the realities of growing up and settling down. Or as the tagline puts it: "A film about growing up . . . relationships . . . marriage . . . and how to avoid all three."

Reviewer Derek Elley noted, "Smart, witty tales of growing up—about that attractively comic moment when adulthood appears on the horizon but childhood still exerts a strong pull—often come from the States, the products of well-fashioned scripts. It is, then, good to report that *The Jolly Boys' Last Stand*—British to its core—is easily in the same league."

The film stars a pre–*Lord of the Rings* Andy Serkis as Spider, the Jolly Boys' Peter Pan in chief who is getting married. Des, Spider's best friend and best man, decides to make a home video about the Boys as a wedding gift—and to remind Spider of the fun he's leaving behind.

When yet another of the group, Vinnie, played by Baron Cohen, also gets engaged, it appears the Jolly Boys' days of carefree youth filled with drinking and pranks are numbered.

Shot in 1998 on digital video, the movie was reportedly made for a paltry £6,000—which would barely cover the Krispy Kreme bill on a studio film. Unable to pay for shooting permits, the filmmakers shot on the run. But the film has a surprisingly polished look and is generally engaging.

Director Payne says the film is less a satire on the party culture of young men than simply a movie that pokes fun.

Sacha's character prepares to videotape having sex with his girlfriend . . . something real girlfriend, Isla, would *never* have allowed.

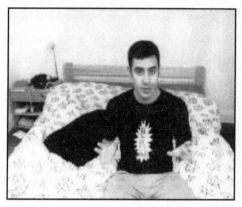

"I think we just wanted to take the mickey* out of the way blokes wear the same sweatshirts, with all the places they've been to, thinking they're so hilarious. I think 'satire' is too strong a word. I like it, though," Payne admits. "It makes us sound like we knew what we were doing."

The casting of the film was a combination of friendly nepotism and chance. Payne had previously met Sacha when he was doing stand-up. After hearing Payne describe the plot of the movie, Baron Cohen suggested including a scene about a couple who videotape each other while in bed. "Immediately," Payne says, "I realized this could be a funny, potentially uncomfortable scene that played to the strengths of video: immediate, raw, recognizably domestic." He adds that Sacha probably didn't realize "I would use *him* to do it."

---

*An abbreviated form of the cockney rhyming slang "take the mickey bliss," meaning "take a piss."

A while later Payne happened to see Andy Serkis in a play called *Mojo*. "His character was a slightly smug, self-important big fish in a small pond, qualities which Spider has."

By this time in the late 1990s, Serkis was considered one of Britain's brightest rising dramatic actors, having carved out a successful theater career as well as appeared in several high-profile television miniseries. Once he was on board, Payne realized he just might be able to get enough financial backing to film his script. "Having Andy turned the project from a soggy house of cards in a shower of disinterest to something which might happen."

They sent the character descriptions to agents, seeking young actors willing to work for profit participation (another way of saying "free") rather than a salary (actual money in the hand). Payne didn't expect more than a handful of responses. "But we were inundated. What we didn't realize at the time was it must have been a dream project for an agent to fob off the daily calls from drama school grads with nothing but an interview for *The Bill** to go to."

For the auditions, Payne admits, he "dreamed up squirmingly embarrassing scenes for people to improvise, and to tell you the truth, you know in two minutes who you are going to cast. I think improvisation is brilliant for testing the

*The Bill* has featured nearly every up-and-coming dramatic actor in guest spots over its run.

speed of an actor's intelligence and comedy relies so much on speed of intention." Rehearsal was like a comedy class exercise. The actors had to answer questions in character and do a lot of improvisation.

Sacha was a shoo-in.

Payne says the film was shot in four weeks using a Digi-beta camera kit. To shoot the film, he enlisted a number of documentary cameramen he knew from his days as a runner. "All the kit, including postproduction services, was given. The biggest expense, I think, was sandwiches."

The production employed guerilla tactics, filming on location across London, from Trafalgar Square to golf country clubs—locales that normally require expensive permits to film. Payne's most vivid memory of the shoot is laughing—a lot. Payne also remembers that the actresses in the film showed Herculean patience.

Without his gangsta wardrobe and knit cap, Sacha looks ~~geekier~~ younger than his television alter ego and

*Jolly Boys* director Christopher Payne was impressed with Sacha's improvisation skills.

there's a self-consciousness about the performance—perhaps because embodying a person as opposed to a caricature felt more personally revealing. At the same time, there's a subtle smugness, the same cleverer-than-thou superiority that would more fully creep into Ali G's persona.

Filmstalker reviewer Richard Brunton was kinder, saying he was "surprised at how Cohen plays his character." While some elements of his well-known characters were evident, Brunton says Sacha "still manages to actually be someone almost normal. However, there is an annoying habit of him picking a space to look at while he delivers his lines that reminded me that he was an actor in a scene again and again."

The DVD includes the casting auditions, offering a unique view into the actors. "Perhaps the most interesting is seeing [Rebecca] Craig act against an offscreen Cohen. It's here that Cohen provides one of his strongest performances and makes me think that these were unscripted—perhaps he copes better off-script?"

*The Jolly Boys' Last Stand* went over well with test audiences, but major distributors were leery. "Our genius marketing strategy was to fill our screenings with people with 'infectious laughs,'" Payne recalls. "The first two were amazing. In the third, our target head honcho came in with a face like a slapped arse and walked after ten minutes—past me in the bar in fact as I bought myself a good-luck bevvy."

Although distributors liked the film, the consensus was it would be a hard sell and therefore financially prohibitive to market. Payne feels *Jolly Boys* was hurt by not being shown at the Edinburgh Festival: "I think we might have got some proper distribution if people had seen how well it went down with an audience."

Two years after the movie was completed, it screened for a week in London. Payne says, "I took my parents to a midweek screening and then I pretty much forgot all about it."

The film came out in 2000 and disappeared in a blink. No matter. Even if Baron Cohen the actor was still an unknown, Ali G certainly wasn't. But Sacha's gain would ultimately be *The 11 O'Clock Show*'s demise. He had left before the start of the fourth series, which began February 15, 2000, and by the end of the year the show would be canceled due to plummeting ratings.

A local paper reported: "The program, hosted by double act Iain Lee and Daisy Donovan, has been in ratings freefall since the departure of spoof rapper Ali G. . . . Last night the cast and crew held a very subdued wrap party to mark the end of filming."

Sacha once joked he planned to "enjoy the trappings of fame, get propositioned for sex by good-looking women, and maybe introduce crack to the showbiz drug scene." And for all anyone knew, he had done just that. His obsession to keep his private life cloaked in mystery at first glance bordered on Howard Hughes paranoia—or "I am an *artiste*" self-indulgence. Some defended that eccentricity as creative prerogative; his critics saw it as a way to avoid confronting the accusations that his comedy had taken a dark turn.

There was a third option—clever manipulation. As an

associate once noted, "I think he is very smart. He knows that Ali G is not going to last and he is going to rake it in while he can. He's incredibly talented but he must know anything he does in the future is *never* going to be as big— it's impossible that it could be."

(Nice call, Nostradamus.)

The associate's lack of prescience aside, the salient point was, Sacha *is* smart—smart enough to plan for a post–Ali G future. Even as *Da Ali G Show* was bringing him fame and fortune and opening countless career doors, Baron Cohen was developing other characters: Bruno the gay fashion reporter, and a newer incarnation of Alexi, now called Borat. Ali G introduced him by commenting, "After watching the free five minutes of the Fantasy Channel, me feel relaxed enough to flick through the other foreign satellite stations," where he came across Borat producing his "Guide to Britain."

Andrew Newman, who worked with Sacha on *Da Ali G Show,* says watching Baron Cohen expand beyond Ali G convinced him Sacha wasn't a one-trick pony. "He totally immerses himself in the characters and becomes them. It means he can interact with people totally naturally and think on the hoof. It goes way beyond acting; it's almost uncanny."

But there were lines even Baron Cohen wouldn't cross. In the opening credits of *Da Ali G Show* is a brief shot of a bare-assed Ali G—except, contrary to what the producers originally claimed, it wasn't Sacha's exposed behind on display. The derriere double was a model named Stephen Jones.

Ali's explanation? "We had to use a body double because me beast is so massive. You couldn't get it on da telly even if you had wide-screen."

Producer Jo Dunn told reporters, "I don't really know why he didn't do it himself. But it's not very comfortable standing around naked in front of a crew. I should imagine the body double has a more perfect physique than his own—and Ali G demands perfection."

While some fans may have been disappointed at Sacha's unwillingness to personally drop his defiant drawers, the fact was, as the years passed, and as Baron Cohen got older, Ali G became less and less a *yoof* satire and more a stand-up with a clever gimmick. And, in fact, in 2001 he went on a seventy-date, twenty-four-venue comedy tour spread out over three months that London's *The People* reported netted the performer over £1.5 million—*after* taxes and expenses.

No wonder he could afford to donate his time to interview David and Victoria (Posh Spice) Beckham at Comic Relief. Upon being introduced, Ali G told the audience: "You is probably thinking, why is I doing Comic Relief? Well . . . Africa is not just a country that gave us Bob Marley. I seen documentaries about it and there is some terrible images that has been left in my mind especially of tribeswomen with well-droopy swingers. With your help we can stop these shocking things happening. . . ."

Posh and Becks

During the interview, Sacha sprawled out in his chair, no longer the buffoon but with the air of a man enjoying an inside joke. Beckham, on the other hand, had the wide-eyed look of a man completely out of his element waiting for disaster to strike, although his wife seemed to mostly enjoy being fodder for Ali G.

|  |  |
|---|---|
| Ali G: | So do you want [your son] to grow up to be a footballer like his dad . . . or a singer like Mariah Carey? |
| Victoria Beckham: | Well, I'm hoping he will grow up to be a footballer like his dad . . . and *I'd* like to grow up and be a singer like Mariah Carey. |
| Ali G: | Respec. We has got to have a break now because Posh is going to do a bit of breast-feeding back- |

stage. Just out of interest . . . is
there one going spare?

In May 2001, Sacha was honored with two British
Academy of Film and Television Awards, or BAFTAs, for
Best Comedy Performance and Best Comedy Program.
The fact that Baron Cohen attended as Baron Cohen prob-
ably says more about the strict dress code of the event than
any show of respect on his part.

When Sacha, dressed in black, accepted his first award,
he told the audience, "Playing the role of Ali G has been
such a challenge. He's such an exuberant fella. If he was
here he would no doubt say something along the lines of
'boyakasha,' or 'respec,' or something like that."

Baron Cohen probably had other words on his tongue
when one of his awards turned up missing at the end of the
ceremony. Organizers of the event searched the venue and
made an announcement over the house system, but no
BAFTA.

A spokesman for the group told the BBC, "It still hasn't
turned up," admitting, "It's not the first time. A couple of
years ago, the Spanish film director Pedro Almodóvar lost
his BAFTA at the film awards—but it was returned the
next day. Hopefully the original will turn up in due course.

"We're sorry that one of his BAFTAs went missing—
but we're glad he was still able to go home with two."
(Two wins . . . one award.)

Sticky fingers also walked off with a pair of £1,000

Jimmy Choo shoes belonging to actress Tracy Shaw. She had taken them off to dance at the post-awards party. According to eyewitnesses, Shaw was irate. At least Sacha had his award replaced by the Academy for free.

However, press reports in *The Mirror* suggested that BAFTA organizers were less than enamored with the comic. "He didn't endear himself with his prima donna behavior." Instead of walking down the red carpet, Sacha snuck in, away from the fans and photographers. He also reportedly threatened to walk out of the press room if anyone tried to ask a question and didn't show up at the official post-awards party.

Even if Sacha had no interest in putting himself out for the media and was intent on keeping himself hidden behind Ali G—he even gave autographs as Ali, not Sacha, in Ali's own handwriting—he didn't shy away from promoting his brother Erran. In addition to hiring Erran to write music for the television series, Sacha showed up at the 2001 MTV Europe Music Awards as Ali G, wearing a cap with the logo "Zohar"—the name of Erran's band.

"He is really positive on the whole about my music and he tells a lot of people about our new album," Erran told *Evening Standard*'s Richard Simpson at the time. Erran added, "For me, not being in the public eye is very important . . . even though I hope our music will attract the same kind of cult following Ali G has."

Actually, Ali G officially passed from cult to mainstream when he was invited to appear on the long-running talk show *Parkinson,* hosted by the gentlemanly Michael Parkin-son. After telling "Parkie" he had never watched the show because it was on opposite *G-String Divas,* Ali G admitted, "Me gotta be honest. Me only came on here as a favor to me nan. She fancies u; she want u bad, Parkinson. She told me she wanna go on a date wit u. I hexpect u to be a perfect gentleman. . . . Unfortunately, *she* don't."

When asked why he shied away from interviews, Ali explained, "That's coz last time me was intraviewed, me ended up getting one hundred hours community service."

Not exactly—but if British parents had gotten their way, he would have.

# 6

# Stirring It Up

**SACHA** BARON **COHEN** parlayed **ALI G** into **AN** estimated £15 million INDUSTRY via **LIVE performances,** the **television** SHOWS, and **FILM** and **VIDEO** SALES.

**IN** February 2002, Ali G was a guest on a BBC's Radio 1 morning show hosted by pert Sara Cox—affectionately known as Coxy. The result: one of the most outrageous radio airings that made tabloid headlines.

Ali was on the show to promote a single he had recorded with reggae/pop crossover star Shaggy called "Me Julie," about his oft talked about girlfriend, which was to be on the sound track of his upcoming movie, *Ali G Indahouse*. The interview turned into a profanity-laced, innuendo-filled rant that appeared premeditated and designed to create a dustup.

The highlights of his half hour on air include Ali G's assertion that he "knobbed" J-Lo; reminiscing about smuggling drugs through customs by hiding them in his rectum; calling singer Will Young a "batty boy":* calling Coxy a "ho" and a

---

*Batty boy: slang for "homosexual." While Young is, in fact, gay, "batty boy" is derisive in tone.

bitch and suggesting she consider "lezzing it" with fellow radio host Zoe Ball; bragging about his big penis; alluding to anal sex and ejaculation; and tossing in a "motherfucker" for good measure.

It was raw enough for Shaggy to comment, "I hope to God my mum isn't listening."

Mums were the least of it—a significant percentage of Coxy's audience is young kids. And during that week schools were on between-term break, so even more kids were tuned in. Although Cox apologized during the program and after, the fallout was still immediate and indignant.

*Daily Mail*'s Linda Lee-Porter expressed naked contempt, calling his appearance little more than "a sick torrent of obscenities. He was vicious, vile, and cruel on a program which is listened to mostly by children." Lee-Porter concluded that it was clear the outburst was "planned, orchestrated and deliberate. He thinks he's a funny, courageous revolutionary smashing down inhibitions and conventions. No doubt he believes that anyone who was shocked is puerile and suburban. . . . Radio 1 has a huge influence on adolescents and the subliminal message they receive day in, day out is that it's smart to be rude and foul. . . . The BBC still has many qualities, but it's time it stopped pandering to the nastiest side of human nature."

The BBC quickly issued a contrite public statement, saying in part: "We are certainly extremely apologetic to any of our listeners and Sara's apology was issued immediately

Coxy sued the *People* newspaper for printing photos of her sunbathing nude in 2001. *British Broadcasting Corporation*

afterwards." Defending Cox by crediting her with trying to control the uncontrollable Ali G, the BBC claimed Baron Cohen had been warned beforehand that swearing is a breach of BBC rules, but conceded, "The difficulty was that it was near-the-knuckle stuff but it was content which is typical of Ali G's style."

That didn't appease John Beyer, Mediawatch director and self-appointed arbiter of "taste and decency in the media." He called the broadcast "an absolute disgrace. These kinds of words are unacceptable day or night. Live interviews with people who have a reputation ought to be more carefully monitored."

Baron Cohen never addressed the issue, but Ali G commented, "So, if this show teach you anything, it should teach you how to respect everyone: animals, children, bitches, spazmos, mingers, lezzers, fatty boombahs, and even gaylords. So, to all you lot watching this, but mainly to the normal people, respect." But that was not to be construed as an apology.

In *The Observer,* Jay Rayner reported: "According to his press people—and he has many these days—Ali G did not apologize for using the word *motherfucker*. It would not be in character to do so. Radio 1 agrees that he didn't but claims that Sacha *did* say sorry to the show's producers." He noted that Ali G's spokeswoman will not comment because "after all she doesn't represent Sacha Baron Cohen. She only represents someone called Ali G. . . ."

A Radio 1 spokesman said, "The regrettable outburst was typical of Ali G's style, despite our talking to him about guidelines," adding that, "Ali feels very sorry about it, too."

*The Independent* commented: "In other words, they behaved as if Ali G were a person, not a creation of a comedian, Sacha Baron Cohen."

Sara Cox confirmed that there was no public mea culpa from Ali G—nor had she particularly expected one. "If you get Ali G, you half know what to expect. For all the fun stuff, [he]'s a bit of a wild card."

It's not that anyone should have been surprised. When Ali hosted the MTV Europe Music Awards, he had censors' ears ringing as the 130-plus countries tuned in Ali in his blue-streak glory. (Among his more amusing comments: When he introduced singer Dido, he encouraged the audience to "big it up for Dildo—strap it on, girl.")

A legal source at MTV said: "We know that the Independent Television Commission is going to come down really hard on us for the content of Ali G's performance. But it is the price we are going to have to pay for letting Sacha Baron Cohen write his own script and not having it [vetted] by our department.

"That was one of his demands which we agreed to—we considered it worth the risk. He said, 'I'm a comedian and I will entertain—but I won't have my work changed.' Fines in cases as severe as this can spiral into hundreds of thousands of pounds—it's no joke."

The Broadcasting Standards Commission (BSC) investigated the Radio 1 flap and determined the Ali G interview was "wholly inappropriate" and criticized Radio 1 for exhibiting a "lack of editorial control," which gave Baron Cohen free rein to run amok.

Lord Dubs of Battersea, chairman of the BSC, said, "The existing control systems clearly didn't work in this case. That is why the commission took a serious view of it, and, most unusually, required the broadcaster to broadcast and publish our finding against the program. We welcome the BBC's decision to amend and strengthen their briefing procedures for live interviews on Radio 1 for the future."

As Lord Dubs alluded, even prior to the commission's report, Radio 1 had scrambled to revise and strengthen their standards and practices, promising "special consideration to live interviews when children are likely to be listening."

Among the steps taken to prevent a second coming of Ali G were that "interviewees will now be warned beforehand on the likelihood that children will be listening." They will also be reminded about the importance of appropriate language and briefed on the stations' guidelines. Any guest who flaunts the rules will be given two warnings.

Another breach will result in the interview being immediately terminated.

What wasn't being said publicly was that BBC executives doubted any amount of oversight would have prevented Ali G's controversial behavior, which seemed to have been carefully premeditated—not to shock young sensibilities but to promote his upcoming feature film, which was to premiere in March. The Radio 1 incident and others kept Ali G's name a fixture in the media the month leading to the movie's release.

The single he had recorded with Shaggy, "Me Julie," made news because it had to be censored. Among the lyrics:

> The people just stared and said it was too long, but
> It ain't crap to have a twelve-inch dong.

And then there was the furor of the movie poster, in which Ali G was crouched beside a naked woman facing away from the camera. His hand is reaching between her legs so he can grab her butt in a suggestive pose.

The Telegraph's Matt Born reported solemnly: "In one of its speediest and most stringent rulings, the Advertising Standards Authority [or ASA] said the poster for the film Ali G Indahouse was widely regarded as offensive and pornographic."

In an official statement released to the press, ASA director Christopher Graham said: "This poster clearly caused serious offense to many who saw it and we have acted promptly to ensure that the image is taken down and stays down." The ASA rebuked the film's producers for using what they deemed a controversial image and sanctioned United International Pictures by requiring the company to submit posters for any film it wants to distribute, regardless of the age of audience, for two years. According to Born, "The ruling reflects the scale of public reaction to the poster. . . . The watchdog received 109 complaints about the advert in just five days after it went up on March 18."

With radio and print scandals successfully under his belt, Baron Cohen set his sights on television. In one notorious commercial, Ali G inadvertently pulls off the Queen's skirt. He looks down between her legs and notes, "Shaven haven—respect!"

The real Queen was not remotely amused. The ads were declared "unfit for TV" and yanked.

While the stunts succeeded in keeping Ali G the talk of swinging London Town, the relentless bad boy act began wearing thin. By the time the movie premiered, the buzz was running neck and neck with media antipathy.

Ali G's movie poster caused sanctions against the production company.

*Ali G Indahouse* was a cross between *Mr. Smith Goes to Washington* and . . . well, *Da Ali G Show*. The basic plot has Ali being elected to Parliament, where he outwits a conniving politician. But the setup simply exists to provide a framework for Ali G to do his stuff.

"It's a classic fish-out-of-water scenario," says Dan Mazer, who cowrote the script:

> We knew that Ali existed best when interviewing stuffy, pompous, self-righteous individuals. And this ridiculous character was best against a framework of seriousness.
>
> Therefore we asked ourselves, "What is the most serious, highfalutin, and austere surrounding in which he can place him?" And that's the world of politics, so the two naturally fit.
>
> Also, because the interviews have basically been around serious issues and are satirical to some degree, we wanted to bring that aspect of his character into the film.

To shoot the movie's opening sequence, the production spent a week filming on location in Los Angeles, to the delight of producer Dan Glazer.

"You've been working away very happily on a script for a bit and you think, *OK, a movie might happen, it might not,* but the thing about films is that everyone says, 'Oh yeah, yeah, yeah,' but ninety percent of films fall through," Glazer says.

"So to walk into the middle of East L.A.—gangstaville, if you please—with a crew of a hundred and ten, shooting a movie, was a bit unreal. It was an amazing experience, and most importantly we all got quite a nice tan," Glazer says, making it sound as if L.A.'s tormented inner city was akin to a Disneyland attraction—a cheery outlook not necessarily shared by anyone who actually lives in "gangstaville."

The film's director, Mark Mylord, admits he was nervous going into the gang-infested area. "I was scared out of my wits," says Mylord, who was making his feature film directorial debut. "We ended up working with the local street gangs . . . as movie extras. They were the nicest guys."

Back in Britain, the filmmakers kept their shooting locations a closely guarded secret. "It all relies on people believing that this person Ali G could actually exist, so when it came to choosing our locations, we really wanted to reflect that world. He's a suburban homeboy, so we had to go to the suburbs and re-create this genuine world of bleakness, almost boredom, in which these people live and thrive."

It was reported that Baron Cohen approached Madonna about a cameo appearance in the film but she politely begged off because of her busy schedule. Some cynics suggested that, being no fool, Madge wasn't about to set herself up to be at the mercy of Ali G. But actresses lined up around the block for the chance to play Ali G's squeeze Julie.

"Julie was the hardest, because everyone had a view of

Tamzin—out *British Broadcasting Corporation*

what she should be like," says director Mark Mylord. "She needed to have a tough element to her, but we also needed to fall in love with her—the girl next door with an edge, yet still with a touch of innocence."

Tamzin Outhwaite, best known for playing Mel on the ageless, enduring soap *EastEnders,*\* was Sacha's first choice to play Julie.

"I've known Sacha Baron Cohen for years," Tamzin says. "He's lovely—we've got the same friends and started in the business at the same time. We used to meet at parties and once we were successful, we'd be like, 'How's it going for you?' 'Yeah, all right. It's a bit weird, isn't it?'

"We both thought it was really funny when he got a call from Madonna's people about the 'Music' video. Madonna's a legend."

But other work prevented Outhwaite from accepting the offer. In the end, the filmmakers cast Kellie Bright,

---

\*Here is an interesting fact about *EastEnders*. It's now on four times a week, with a marathon showing of the week's episodes aired on Saturday. One of the highest-rated shows ever on, *EastEnders* averages a 45–50 percent audience share in Britain—every week. That's a higher percentage of viewers than watch the Academy Awards in the United States.

Kellie—in

who seemed to spend much of the movie engaged in "tonguing sessions" with bf Ali G.

"The kissing thing, as with so much of it, was thrown in at the last moment," Bright says. "The first time we kissed was my first day on set, and initially we did a kind of playground kiss that was pretty innocent. Then Sacha and Mark disappeared for half an hour, and Mark came back and said could we try something different. 'Could you tongue each other?' And I asked, 'What? Outside my mouth?' So that's what we did.

"After we'd slobbered over each other each time," Kellie says, "I had to have my entire facial makeup reapplied."

There were also some tense wardrobe moments. While filming was going on, someone snuck into Sacha's trailer and stole a television, a DVD player, a video recorder, and several of Ali G's signature custom-made tracksuits, prompting one crew member to comment, "Whoever stole it isn't exactly going to be able to walk down the street unnoticed."

When the production filmed in Staines, it was a surreal fusion of fact and fiction. Dan Mazer was fascinated that people in Staines still think Ali G is real, apparently not at all troubled by the notion of confusing fiction with reality.

Tongues—both out

"They come up to him and say, 'You live next door to my cousin, don't you!' Someone actually said, 'Your mum's buried next to mine in Staines Cemetery.' It's like they don't know the distinction between the character and the actor. They think Ali G is Ali G but he puts on a different voice to become the character. It's like Sacha Baron Cohen doesn't even exist."

Yeah, well . . . and whose doing is that?

No matter. Staines's city fathers saw Ali G as a way to put their town on the tourist map by promoting its most famous non-existent son. According to *The Telegraph*, Staines's city council

> is to produce brochures highlighting Staines' significance as the birthplace and continued residence of the comic character, who was educated locally and claims membership of the West Staines Massive street gang.
>
> Officials at Spelthorne borough council say their decision to include Ali G in their *tourism strategy* follows the arrival of tourists trying to

locate "landmarks" such as the Crooked Billet Roundabout and the KFC fast-food outlet [that was to be featured in the film].

A council spokesman explained, "I think it is right to use him in future tourism brochures—he is something we can use very positively and he has increased the awareness of the town a lot."

So they were certainly rooting for *Indahouse* to keep the Ali G gravy train chugging along. And the Staines city council members weren't the only ones hoping to attract the spotlight via Ali G. British television legend and ego extraordinaire Sir Jimmy Savile chose the occasion of *Indahouse*'s release to give an interview to *The Sun* announcing that Baron Cohen owed all his success to him, Jimmy. Or, more to the point, that Sacha "stole his act."

Savile has been around for fifty years, starting as a radio show host. From 1975 to 1994 Jimmy hosted the ridiculously popular *Jim'll Fix It,* in which he "fixed it" so that people's wishes came true, and he was *Top of the Pops* host for its first twenty years. Along the way he authored several books, recorded a hit record, and is an accomplished marathon runner.

He also owns a mountain, is a lifelong bachelor, lived with his mother—the Duchess—all his adult life, and since her death has kept her bedroom as a shrine and has her clothes regularly dry-cleaned. Yes, Jimmy Savile is quite the eccentric.

Savile has claimed that Baron Cohen had made his fortune thanks to him. "If I wasn't here, he would be skint." Savile also pointed out that the tracksuits and bulky jewelry Ali G wears is just like what he (Savile) wore on TV back in 1961. "He must go to the charity shops I give my old tracksuits to," he complained.

Few gave much credence to Sir Jimmy's claims. However, according to artist/author Harland Miller, Savile very well might have been an inspiration—not for Ali G per se but for what became hip-hop style.

While looking through Jimmy's autobiography, *Love Is an Uphill Thing,* Harland notes, "In nearly all the pictures he wore tracksuits coupled with chunky gold jewellery [sic]. As I fanned through his career, the tracksuits became more flamboyant (handmade, in fact), the jewellery bigger, the look darker, meaner, with wraparound shades." The book Miller perused was autographed. "Even the signature struck me as very rap: He used a pound sign for the *J* of 'Jimmy' and a dollar sign for the *S* of 'Savile': £$."

On the back cover was a picture of Savile leaning on a Rolls-Royce. "He was wearing a flashy tracksuit, and it looked as if he had redeemed every pledged gold chain from every pawnshop in Leeds and put it round his neck."

Sir Jimmy harbors no hard feelings—quite the contrary. "I think it's a tribute to me," he says, taking Ali G's signature look as a flattering homage, just one of the many he claims to have enjoyed over the decades. "Comedians have been doing me for forty years." Savile has suggested

> "I must be the most impersonated person ever. Only I could have entered two Jimmy Savile look-alike contests and come in fourth and last."

that Baron Cohen could make up for it by sending along "a few quid and a few cigars."

Despite the publicity Sir Jimmy generated with the story, Sacha's camp remained mute on the claims. They had a movie to open. The film's premiere took place at the Empire Theatre in Leicester Square in late March 2002. Ali donned a thirty-foot velvet cape with a crown perched on his head. Accompanying him were six more-than-naked women wearing strategically placed cloth marijuana leaves. He explained his girlfriend's absence. "I told me Julie that the premiere was tomorrow night coz I knew there would be loads of bitches here tonight."

Before the start of the film, Ali spoke to the star-studded, but royal-family-light audience. "The Queen and Charles said no. And Harry said no—probably coz him still owe me twenty squid for dat eight. . . . I must thank Working Title Films for this. They forked out twelve million pounds for the movie. And eleven-point-five million pounds went into that café in Amsterdam."

*The Mirror*'s Jessica Callan reported that for all the carefully planned choreography, there was one thing Baron Cohen didn't anticipate:

When Sacha arrived dressed as Ali G and attended by six thong-clad babes, his mum,
Daniella, raced over. And, for a few marvelous
moments, she punctured his entire act. Eyes
down, the embarrassed-looking star mumbled a
few words in his natural North London accent
before sweeping off to resume his increasingly
tiresome Ali posturing.

Making a feature film: £3.5 million. Throwing a lavish
premiere party: £250,000. Having Mum ruin your big
entrance: priceless.

Not only did all his family, friends, and fans show up, so
did protesters carrying signs that read: *Don't Call Me
Nigger, Racism Ain't Funny,* and *Al Jolson Go Home.*

Ali responded by joking, "It's clear there's a lot of
racialism out there and if they see a brother onscreen and
they knock me for that then so be it. Keep it real."

Blacks weren't the only ones using the premiere as an
opportunity to bring attention to their grievances. The
previous week the Web site jewish.co.uk had posted an
open letter to Baron Cohen, in essence shunning him

until he learns to be less insulting to others and
stops behaving like a *schmuck.*

Now is the time for you to act like a *mensch*
and if you have any respect for others just shut
your mouth up and work on something new. As

a Cohen, you should realize that it's all about leadership and role models. What sort of values are you giving to young Jews?

Certainly not much as living in a diverse society is not about insulting others. How would you start feeling if the joke was Jewish, and had carried on for as long as Ali G has? You too would start feeling a bit sick and tired of it.

Typically, Sacha seemed impervious to criticism and carried on. The after-party was held at the Mayfair Club, where, keeping true to form, Sasha refused to speak to the press as himself. The conceit was clearly wearing thin.

"Will the real Sacha Baron Cohen please stand up?" wrote one exasperated reporter in *The Mirror,* calling the premiere party for *Ali G Indahouse* "a bizarre insight into the schizophrenic world of Mr B. C." and complaining that the movie's star refused to talk to journalists as himself. "It's all very clever creating a hilarious character like Ali, but not if you let your alter ego take over your life."

Declining to have his photograph taken, Baron Cohen reportedly huddled in a corner with his advisors instead. Sacha's mother and father, Gerald and Daniella, spoke briefly to the press and expressed their parental pride . . . as well as their reticence to say more. "You must remember, he's the boss and although we have had a great night, we're not allowed to say we have, unless we have okayed it with Sacha."

How ~~creepy~~ sweet is that?

Apparently, though, Sacha loosened the gag order long enough for his mom to tell the *Daily Mail,* "To be honest I expected it to be worse, but our son had warned us it would be rude. I found it very funny and I was very pleased to be there."

Gerald added, "My wife had to explain some of it to me, but once I knew what was going on I found it funny—far funnier than I had expected."

When asked about the scantily clad women parading around the premiere, the elder Baron Cohen laughed. "I expected a lot worse."

Reviews were generally tepid. Christopher Tookey of the *Daily Mail* pronounced *Ali G Indahouse* a lazy and obnoxious work. "The film resembles a collection of half-baked sketches assembled by someone with attention deficit syndrome. The impression is of a man cynically determined to cater for the masses, and make his humour as revolting as possible. . . . I came out angry and deeply depressed."

BBC reviewer Neil Smith observed that while the film has plenty of laughs, "some viewers, however, might feel discomfited by the way his sexist, homophobic buffoon has started to embody the very attitudes Cohen originally set out to parody."

Smith goes on to note, "The relentlessly scatological set-pieces—which range from sex with animals to Queen

Elizabeth's pudenda—would make a horny schoolboy blush, and make the BBFC's 15 certificate* hard to fathom." Still, he then goes on to say that the humor is harmless.

In *The Guardian,* Peter Bradshaw called it "an entertaining venture with energy, fun and immature bad taste in abundance."

But even before the premiere ended, it seemed as if Baron Cohen and his collaborators had their sights set three thousand miles to the west, having already screened the film before American test audiences.

"We expected it to go down to deathly silence," Mazer admits. "But while obviously there were parts that totally passed them by, they laughed massively and what they got, they *really* got. . . .

"They'd be coming out of the screenings and saying, 'So like he's a gangsta but like from England, like wow, it's like *Dude, Where's My Car?* . . . but, like, better!' That was the ultimate accolade for us!"

But Mazer acknowledged that pop culture adoration was a moving target with a limited life span. "The character keeps

---

*The British movie rating system has eight categories: U and U$_c$ (universal and suitable for children under four years old); PG (considered safe for children eight and older); 12A (suitable for twelve and over); 12 (no one under twelve admitted without an adult); 15 (suitable for fifteen years and older); 18 (no one under eighteen admitted); R18 (your basic porno, only shown in specially licensed theaters or sex shops).

Mr. Blobby

mutating," he commented in an interview with *The Birmingham Post*. "But when everyone starts saying, 'Oh, God, here he is again,' then that's when we'll stop. We don't want to become Mr. Blobby!"

What Sacha *did* want was to conquer America.

# 7
# Undercover Lover

**IF** YOU **AIN'T** CAREFUL, sex **CAN** lead **TO** some **terrible things:** herpes, SQUAT ROT, **or even worse—SOMEFING CALLED** "A RELATIONSHIP." **—Ali G**

**ON** New Year's Eve 2002, two mortally depressed Israeli youths intruded on Sacha's carefully controlled privacy.

According to the *Daily Mail,* "Comedy star Ali G narrowly escaped injury yesterday during a double suicide at a luxury hotel in Israel." Staying in a £300-a-night suite at the Intercontinental in Tel Aviv, "the entertainer woke up . . . to find bullet holes in the wall and window. He rang hotel security, who called the police."

An Intercontinental spokesman told reporters, "Ali G . . . said he thought he heard shooting last night but didn't think anything of it. It was only this morning when he drew back the curtain that he saw the bullet hole in the window."

The bodies of two cousins, young men aged eighteen and twenty-four, were discovered in an adjoining room. Police determined the youths had killed themselves in a suicide pact—using an M16 assault rifle. Apparently, the first shot went awry and penetrated the connecting wall to Baron Cohen's room, then went out the window.

Most of the British papers ran screaming headlines about Sacha's brush with death, the stories filled with details of the suicides. Buried in the coverage was an unexpected glimpse into Sacha's private life—he had told police he was in Israel to visit family members, including his brother Amnon, and was traveling with girlfriend Isla Fisher.

Even though they had been a couple for close to a year, very little was known about their relationship. Although they began dating in early 2000, neither Fisher nor Baron Cohen would even say where they met. Of course for Sacha this was simply business as usual—for as entrenched in the public eye as Ali G was, Baron Cohen remained deep undercover. Every now and then a random report would surface—dates with Greek actress Zeta Graff, a flirtation with Gwyneth Paltrow—but the impression was that Sacha was either a confirmed bachelor discreetly playing the field or a closed-off genius whose primary intimate relationship was with his hand.

That changed in early 2002 when Sacha-and-Isla sightings became a regular occurrence. In February, the couple were spotted shopping for a new bed in London. Reports that the couple were living together were not exactly confirmed—but there was no denial, either. She was with him for the *Ali G Indahouse* premiere and actually spoke to the press briefly, referring to Sacha as her boyfriend. And when it was announced Baron Cohen was taking Ali G on the road to

America with a new HBO series, it was confirmed Isla would be going with him to Los Angeles.

So who was this five-three redheaded spitfire who had snared one of Britain's most eligible, not to mention most wealthy, bachelors?

Scottish by heritage, Isla (EYE-lah) Lang Fisher was born on February 3, 1976, in Muscat, Oman, the only sister to four brothers. A few years later her father, a banker who worked with the United Nations, relocated his family to Australia, settling in a well-heeled suburb outside of Perth. Isla says she can't remember a time when she didn't want to act. As a young girl she admits to being "the queen of the one-woman show with a need to be the center of attention and rope my brothers into performing with me.

"I basically had ears this size when I was two and I didn't grow into them, so I tended to make people laugh and muck around, which was always fun."

Fisher admits she was inspired by her mom, who was actively involved in local amateur theater productions.

"She was doing *Twelfth Night* and I wasn't allowed to go to a performance, because it was too late at night when they finished," Isla recalls. "But I'd see Mum in her dressing room beforehand and I think a part of me felt I'd missed out on something magical that was happening in the evenings. I think that piqued my interest."

Her mom, Elspeth Reid, says Isla found an agent by browsing through the phone book. "Every day after school, she would ring to see if there was any work."

Isla began acting in commercials when she was nine—around the time her parents divorced—and in 1993 appeared in the Australian television miniseries *Bay Cove,* also known as *Bay City.* Even as a teenager, Fisher was focused on career goals. Her friend Liz Stanley, who met Isla during that time, describes her as having "a very strong personality—she knows what she wants and she goes after it, whether that's men or jobs. From the minute you meet her, you sense that she will do whatever it takes to fulfill her ambitions and goals."

Her *Bay City* costar Michael Muntz has fond memories. "She was lots of fun, always professional and the sort of person you enjoy working with," he says. "She played my fifteen-year-old daughter—she looked much younger than her true age, which was seventeen. But she was wise far beyond her years."

That same year she was cast in *Paradise Beach,* set around three young teenagers who "leave the drabness of the suburbs for Paradise Beach, in search of sun, surf and fun, where relationships are quickly established and friendships formed." In September 1994, Fisher became a regular on the long-running Australian soap *Home and Away,* set in the coastal town of Summer Bay.

The series made Isla, playing Shannon Reed, a household name—as the poster child of teenage angst. But her character certainly made an attention-grabbing entrance: When Shannon and her brother Chris arrived in Summer Bay, town residents were shocked, *shocked,* to discover the sibs

Why is this man smiling? Isla looks like she's just realized that's *not a* seashell in his pocket. . . .

were romantically involved. Relief all the way round when it was revealed they were only adopted brother and sis.

Over the next three years Shannon battled anorexia, flirted with a lesbian affair that was boringly never consummated, dated an abusive fitness trainer, had an affair with an older man, found her birth mother, and finally left for Paris.

Offscreen Isla was equally busy. During her stint on the show she wrote two teenage romance novels—*Seduced by Fame* and *Bewitched*. In 1997, *FHM* readers voted her onto the 100 Sexiest Women in the World list.

Not everyone was so enamored. Costar Nick Freedman was quoted as calling her "a silly little redhead. The best bit was when I had to act blind because I didn't have to see her."

*Meow!*

Her friend Liz Stanley acknowledges that Isla's ambition was fueled by a healthy ego. It was inevitable her ambition would lead her away from Australia. "After four years of soap fame and being in the limelight," Isla says, "I thought it was time to have some training so I might have longevity in my career."

Fisher admits few of her peers supported her decision, because she was getting offers to work in Australian films. "But I left because it was a gut instinct."

She saw the move as just another step of her career and in a 1998 interview explained, "I've worked non-stop since I was twelve, in Perth, Western Australia. When I was sixteen I left home to do *Paradise Beach* in Queensland. And when I was nineteen I moved on to *Home and Away* in Sydney."

However, her decision to move to London wasn't *entirely* career based. It was also where her boyfriend, record producer Anthony de Rothschild, happened to live. Her plan was to take a year off to train and to live in Paris, where she had enrolled in the Jacques Lecoq mime school.* Isla would commute to London on weekends to see Rothschild.

In retrospect, Fisher believes the move was brave and admits it was a very difficult time. "I'd arrived in England a couple of months before I started and I was seeing . . . Anthony, who meant a lot to me." Unfortunately, they broke up right before she was set to move to Paris, leaving Isla on her own.

After having spent much of her youth on television in Australia, she was a complete unknown in France. Rather than miss fame, Fisher says it made her realize something:

*Jacques Lecoq was Philippe Gaulier's teacher and mentor, Gaulier being the man Sacha credits his career to.

"I don't want to be defined by my work. I learned that I wasn't going to place my self-worth in something external, or be graded by other people's opinions. Bloody hell, I'm not going to be judged!"

In 1998, Isla described herself as "fiery. I don't sit on the fence. I say what I mean and say what I feel. It's very Australian. No bullshit." And one of her favorite topics was the press and her aversion to giving interviews because, she claims, she is "always misquoted. It's so easy for the tone of something to read differently from how you intended it, or to use the wrong word when you're tired or nervous or eager to please. I became famous quite young doing *Home and Away,* so when you're growing up, when you have a bad hairstyle or a feisty moment or you're going through a phase, you do it in public."

Obviously, it was not a lesson well learned. She returned to Britain in May 1998 and soon got the opportunity to show off her newly acquired performing skills when she was cast in a musical, *Summer Holiday,* opposite popular stage star Darren Day.

By December, the two were engaged after Day proposed during a holiday in the Maldives. It wasn't Fisher's first high-profile romance—besides Rothschild she had been involved with Australian model and television host Nathan Harvey and actor Dan Falzon. But her engagement made her a British tabloid darling, and she seemed more than willing to wax poetic.

"We're probably looking at getting married mid–next

year," she announced in *The Mirror*. "It's up to me to get organized, to get it together. We'll definitely have a celebration in Australia and one here for Darren's family."

She took the opportunity to take issue with press reports that had claimed Isla was the fifth woman he'd been engaged to:

> Although I suppose it's nothing new being victims of hurtful things in the Press, I do find it very, um, distressing. I find it distressing for Darren. I feel for him because he has to bear the brunt of it. To be honest, I'd be concerned if my fiancé at 30 hadn't ever had another relationship.

She was especially miffed that their engagement was leaked to the press:

> We had no intention of telling anyone. When the story broke, it put me in the most horrendous situation because I had phone calls from my friends all around the world, saying: "My God, Isla, you got engaged and you never told me."

Fisher found it unfair and hurtful, but made it clear she didn't see herself as a victim. "I never will be a victim! . . . And at the end of the day, you know, we're all just people trying to get through. And frankly, life's too short to give a shit."

That said, by the summer of 1999, the couple had split and the engagement ended. A humbled Fisher admitted, "I'm always falling for guys who don't love me back. I have been hurt or hurt myself so many times that I have become a pretty tough cookie. But I want to find a relationship that works."

Or at least a partner who didn't kiss and tell. Shortly after her engagement was made public, former boyfriend Nathan Harvey revealed intimate details about their sex life to *The People*. After throwing in a couple of compliments to sweeten his tell-all (she "had a fantastic figure that most women would kill for"), Harvey ended by saying, "I wish her every success."

No wonder the woman is gun-shy with the press . . . and has developed an "I Am Woman, Hear Me Roar" attitude. When asked once if she was a romantic, Isla shrugged. "Who knows." Then, in the summer of 2002, she told *Sunday Mirror* reporter Louise Hancock, "I love the power women have. I think women rule the world because they rule men. Manipulating men—that's our job. That's what we're on the planet for."

She related the story of how as a teenager she broke up with her boyfriend after losing her virginity to him a few hours earlier:

"I wanted to break up with him but I'd never had sex

and I thought, *What a waste,*" she explained. "I'd gone out with him for eight months and I thought I may as well have him. So we did it there and then. And I've been doing that ever since . . . very successfully."

Who knows if that comment gave Sacha pause, but it prompted Hancock to caustically observe, "According to friends, all Isla's exes share one distinctive quality—an uncanny ability to propel her into the limelight. . . . Isla was always determined that she would be world-famous—and it looks as though she is well on the way to realizing her childhood dream. She now has a high-profile lover with plenty of street cred."

After she hooked up with Baron Cohen, Fisher's film career enjoyed an uptick with roles in *Scooby-Doo*, *The Wannabes*, *Dallas 3621,* and *I ♥ Huckabees*. But her breakthrough role was in the 2005 comedy *Wedding Crashers*. In the film she plays Gloria, who decides she has to have Vince Vaughn's Jeremy. Despite his efforts to douse her obsession, she bulls her way into his room, ties him up, and proceeds to have her way with him.

In the scene, Gloria is gloriously nude. Isla, however, isn't. The breasts on view belong to a body double.

"I negotiated that from the beginning, trying to analyze why," Fisher says, "because there's nothing more peaceful and beautiful. After all, we're all born naked, and I totally kind of hate the puritanical approach to the whole nudity thing, but then when it comes to me . . . I'm like double standards—no way am I doing anything like *that,* and it wasn't because of my relationship or because of my parents. It was a personal choice that I just made."

Fisher says it was as much a creative decision as a personal statement. "I didn't think there was anything funny about seeing a woman's nipple. I feel like if you have a female comic character and then you see her nipples, then she is no longer funny, which is clearly wrong, but that was my theory and that's why I didn't want to do it."

Isla also admitted the love scene was uncomfortable for her. "It's always hard. You have a moment where you feel slightly prudish, even though you have a body double and it's playing and pretend. It's not even like it's a drama. But . . . it's a tough thing to do because . . . even though it's a character . . . it's your sexuality." (Or lack thereof. . . .)

*Wedding Crashers* earned Fisher some of her best reviews as a film actress; she feels she has found a niche as a comedic actress and credits Baron Cohen for nudging her in that direction.

Even in school, she was the class clown. Isla says, "I have always been the one to make a fool out of myself to get a laugh at a party or wherever I have been in my life, but I have never really associated that with doing it publicly in such a large arena. But then Sacha was like, 'You are so funny, you are the funniest woman I know—you should be doing comedy.'"

Isla's pregnancy rumors started swirling in March 2007 after photos seemed to reveal a bulging stomach. Rumors proved true—the couple were looking forward to a winter 2007-2008 birth.

While she and Sacha are similar in that "I don't have many boundaries on what I'll joke about in my personal life. I'll say anything that I think is funny," Isla stresses, "I don't like racist jokes." Or the idea of naked wrestling. "I'm quite happy to steer clear of getting suffocated by a naked man sitting on my face."

After *Wedding Crashers,* Fisher's stock rose and she has worked steadily, going from film to film. "Since I started doing what I like to do on camera, I have had a lot more success, so it is interesting," she notes. "When you try to suppress yourself and be really serious, people just don't buy it. It is very different being approached for something that you are proud of having done like *Wedding Crashers,* which I really put myself on the line for."

The movie also made Fisher more recognizable on the street—usually to her dismay. "I've had a lot of women come up to me and say, 'Oh my God, that character you played in *Wedding Crashers*—that's me!' I'm always creeped out, because what was amusing about that character was how absurdly mad she was. She had no social etiquette at all, so when people proudly confess to relating to her, I always think that's weird."

Contrary to the perception that she is driven by ambition, Isla insists she has no master plan. "I am honestly not trying to have some contrived career where I implement a strategy," she said. "I just don't believe in any of that. I like to try to stay true to being an artist and do stuff that really appeals to me, whatever attracts me for whatever reason, whether it is the cast or the script or something that just makes my heart sing."

Her latest coup was being cast in *The Simpsons Movie,* although she could not say what exactly her role was. "They make you sign these terrifying confidentiality agreements, six pages of it. I was nervous. I think I'm allowed to say I'm in it. Maybe I'm not even allowed to say that." It turns out she probably wishes she hadn't said anything, because her role was cut out of the final version.

Gag orders and confidentiality agreements aside, life is good for Isla Fisher. "I am someone who loves what I do and I feel really lucky to be here. I just want to do jobs that make me happy and not try to plan for something that would just ruin my privacy anyway."

Well, what's left of it. The British papers have openly speculated on the couple's lack of urgency to exchange vows. And as their relationship has stretched into a multi-year state of marital limbo, reporters repeatedly tried, and failed, to nail Fisher down. Her evasiveness seems less a

Isla Fisher with
Andy Samberg in
*Hot Rod*

quest for privacy than it does avoidance. Although it's been widely reported Fisher has agreed to convert to Judaism, not much else seems settled.

"If you're after details, you're going to be disappointed." Fisher laughs, admitting she hasn't given it a whole lot of thought. "I'm not making a joke at all when I say that it's not something that I look forward to. And I hear that it's quite hard work. All I know is that I've ruled out wearing fairy wings. When I was nine I wanted to get married in fairy wings, and now I realize that's not cool anymore."

Fisher recalls the time her mother asked her what kind of dress she wanted. "I was like, 'Mum, let's talk about it at another juncture, because I don't know! I need more time.'" While filming *Wedding Crashers,* Isla said several people asked about her wedding plans. "I felt like such a schmuck as I didn't have any answers. Not even funny ones."

She's careful to stress that it's no reflection of her

commitment to Sacha. "While I am a hopeless romantic and excited to spend life with my man, the details you have to deal with. . . . In the back of my mind I think I should be more gung ho about it. I should be more excited about getting it going. I'm sure that it's just that I'm working so hard," she offers, adding, "Yes, that's what I'm going with."

One thing she does know—she has no plans to work with Sacha. "It wasn't that effective for Nicole and Tom Cruise on *Eyes Wide Shut,* was it?" she asks dryly. "I really don't think that's a good idea. . . . It seems to be like the kiss of death for couples, you know? I wouldn't want to tempt fate no matter how tempting having fun together in a movie might be."

While in Oz promoting *Wedding Crashers* in 2005, Fisher—who confessed to being hungover from the previous night's premiere party—sounded homesick and less than sold on staying in Britain to raise a family.

"We don't know when we're getting married but it will definitely be here—coming back this time I realize how attached I am to this place.

"I come back [to Australia] and I'm like: 'Why did I leave here?' Now I am kind of stuck in England and it is a shame. I am going to have kids and push them in an urban area with concrete swings. It's going to be hell."

The cynical among us might read something into that comment.

But other than that momentary crack, Isla has been the

picture of domestic contentment. At the London premiere of *Scooby-Doo* she was there by herself. When asked where her fiancé was, she replied, "He's not here. I don't know where he is."

The cynical among us might wonder why Baron Cohen wasn't by Fisher's side on *her* big night. But later, when cornered by a columnist, she declined to discuss Sacha, other than to say, "I can tell you that I'm happy and very much in love. But my private life is private."

The reporter wrote that they were interrupted by Sacha calling Fisher's cell phone. Isla's side of the conversation was brief: "I love you, darling. . . . Trust me, I'll be home in an hour. . . . I promise."

At least she found out where he was.

And, in a few months, so would America.

# 8

# Across the Pond

> **LET'S** talk **ABOUT** some **CONSPIRACY** things. **LET'S GO** back **TO** the grassy knoll. . . .Who actually shot **J.R.?** —Ali G

**HBO** has never been shy about pushing traditional broadcasting limits. Even the premium channel's slogan—"It's not television; it's HBO"—offers subscribers the tacit promise of daring, intriguing programming. So for HBO executives *Da Ali G Show* was a natural fit.

In Britain, Baron Cohen enjoyed massive popular appeal and had built a huge fan base. But that very success had seriously crimped his comedic freedom. So even though he would have to prove himself to the American audience, being anonymous meant he could unleash Ali G onto unsuspecting targets that were not yet in on the joke.

His guerrilla tactics remained largely unchanged from his early work on *The 11 O'Clock Show*. A *New York Times* reporter followed some of the show's production staff as they sought to arrange an interview. Upon entering the office building, one member of the undercover squad cautioned, "Make sure you don't mention what we're doing in the halls. We're not supposed to even mention Ali G's name."

On the sign-in sheet, the staffer listed United World Productions as her affiliation. Such a company does not exist, but apparently, none of the people invited to appear on the show bothered to check. Although Mazer and Baron Cohen always refused to say exactly how they pulled their ruse off—"It's like David Blaine telling you how he levitates," Mazer explained to writer Neil Strauss—James Baker revealed that he had been sent several letters on United World Productions stationery inviting the former secretary of state to participate in a television series being shot for Britain's Channel 4. The program was supposed to be a six-part look at the American Constitution, aimed at British youth.

It was basically the same tactic guests on the U.K. version of the show described. But what was different was the way guests were chosen. In Britain, Mazer says, people were chosen on the basis of their accent: "If they had an upper-class accent, then the juxtaposition of that with Ali G would be funny." That, however, would not work in America because accents aren't intrinsically tied to social standing. So instead they looked for "pomposity, whether it's liberal or conservative, artistic or scientific."

And nobody was considered off-limits, no scenario too uncomfortable for Baron Cohen to pursue. "He always just had chutzpah—no fear in whatever scenario," says Mazer. "He's more unwilling to take no for an answer than anyone I've ever met. . . . His great skill is his unbelievable tenacity. And he's frustratingly always right."

Well, almost always. Mazer, who tends to pick the targets, admits that Baron Cohen had some high-flying ideas
about who he could get on the show. Included in his wish
list were George Bush and Bill Clinton. Mazer patiently
explained to his creative partner that it wasn't very likely
that the sitting president would clear his schedule for a sit-
down chat with Ali G. "But it doesn't matter if the targets
are old or young, right-wing or left-: It's all about punctur-
ing pomposity."

It was also all about image. An important part of Ali G's
persona is tied to his fashion sense. So joining the staff for
their American adventure was stylist and costume designer
Jason Alper, who first met Baron Cohen back in 1996
through mutual friends. Alper recounted to the *Evening Standard* Baron Cohen's original description of the character:
" 'White guy from the suburbs. Grew up watching rap on
MTV. Massive identity crisis. Thinks he's black and essentially a fool.' And I thought—'ere we go!"

It wasn't so much about making up a look but adopting
one. "Those guys are ridiculous," says Alper, referring to
the bling-covered rap artists. "They carry diamond-
studded canes and drink from twenty-four-carat-gold gob-
lets with the word 'player' inscribed on them and think
they look the business."

Alper started at the top—literally. He selected wraparound sunglasses and a knit skullcap. Then he completed
the above-the-neck ensemble by suggesting Sacha grow a
goatee. Next came the wardrobe. From the start, Alper

envisioned the Ali G character in "a massive tracksuit. So I went to 125th Street in Harlem, a very hip-hop area, and saw a shop with a cow-print tracksuit in the window and said, 'Aye aye.'"

He ordered two suits—one in yellow vinyl, the other a zebra print—and Ali G came to life. Relatively speaking, Alper rarely gets public recognition for his contribution, but his input has been an integral part of Ali G's development.

"The dafter the inspiration, the better the result," Alper says, "and anyone who's six feet three wearing a yellow vinyl tracksuit is gonna look ridiculous." However, in a rather telling statement about the entertainment industry, wherever Baron Cohen and his crew showed up, Ali G was treated as if he really were a famous gangsta. "I get so much enjoyment being paid to fool people. When we have the film in the can, we usually walk away, laughing our heads off."

Mazer and Baron Cohen spent four months in America, filming all across the country. In January 2003, Mazer told the *Daily Mail* that he felt the show being filmed for HBO had better material than the British version. "We've got some really big names and the interviews are hilarious." It was also creatively refreshing that few people in the United States had ever heard of Ali G, so the element of surprise was once again a big part of the show—something that was no longer possible in the U.K.

Leisure time in
the Hebrides
© Sam Maynard

Mazer acknowledged that Ali G had become a ubiqui-
tous part of British culture. "Unless we went to the Outer
Hebrides* and interviewed a man who'd spent his life
living in a cave, we couldn't have done another interview
in Britain, so it's great to be able to take the character to
America."

In Philadelphia Ali G went through the training for
police department recruits. When a crime expert told him
that Hondas were the easiest car to break into, he asked,
"So for young kids out there, would you recommend them
starting with a Honda?"

During New York's Fashion Week, Bruno talked a
model at the Lloyd Klein showing into lending him a pair
of the designer's underwear, then proceeded to flounce his
way down the runway.

Former U.S. attorney general Richard Thornburgh was
one of Ali G's first ~~easy targets~~ guests. After introducing

*The Outer Hebrides are known in the Scottish parliament as the Western Isles.

Thornburg, Ali G proceeds to ask when is it legal to murder someone.

At that moment Thornburgh looks as if he has just realized he's fallen down the rabbit hole. "Never."

"What if they call your mum a ho? Is it all right to murder them then?"

"You can't use as a defense any kind of verbal provocation," Thornburgh explains patiently.

"What if they say your mum is a ho and I know 'cause I done it with her? Surely then you can pop a cap in their ass."

Thornburgh agreed that calling anyone's mom a ho was a terrible thing. "But you can't take another's life for slander."

"Then what if they say it about your nan?"

John Judge, director of the Washington Peace Center, participated on a panel discussing corporate control of U.S. media. He says he was paid for his appearance and was informed the program would be seen by 4 million Britons.

"I'm amazed it even aired," he says. "It was perhaps the most surreal interview I have ever done."

Among the highlights was Ali G asking the panelists why anyone still read books when TV was everywhere. When Judge commented he had read thousands of books, Ali G reprimanded him for showing off and demanded Judge name one to prove it.

"In the final analysis," Judge concluded, "either this fellow is as dumb as a box of rocks" or "he was, as they say, just having us on."

Ali G's interview with Beltway insiders showed what Americans have long known: Politicians are frequently out of touch. Although he was gracious enough when asked if a death-row inmate could avoid execution by having an all-you-can-eat buffet for his final meal, Ed Meese,* attorney general under Ronald Reagan, seemed mostly befuddled, admitting, "He was talking in an argot† with which I am not familiar." (Is it me or does Ali G make more sense than Meese?)

On occasion, the interviews were more silly than satiric. Former United Nations secretary-general Boutros Boutros-Ghali seemed amused when Ali G asked, "What's the funniest language, mon? French, innit?"

"Not necessarily," the diplomat said, and considered a moment. "Maybe Arabic is more funny. It depends to whom."

Newt Gingrich, who was never at a loss for words when Speaker of the House, was rendered mute during this exchange with Ali G, who first asked him if America would ever elect a female president. Gingrich said he believed the country would, eventually.

---

*Meese is best known for his 1986 attack on pornography. He singlehandedly got convenience stores to remove all men's magazines such as *Playboy* until a federal court reminded him of a little detail called the First Amendment and stopped the purge.

†Argot: slang, vernacular, jargon, patois.

| Ali G: | Aren't you worried that she will spend all her time shopping for shoes and getting facials? |
|---|---|
| Gingrich: | No, I don't think that would be a danger. |
| Ali G: | Yeah, but what if she fell in love with Saddam Hussein? Because we all know that women love a bastard.* |

Although a spokesman for Gingrich declined to make an official comment, *Time Online* reported that one of his staff shrugged it off. "They got us, ha ha, we're amused. So what? Move on."

Ali G's interviews also showed what Americans have additionally long known: The Catholic Church and Ralph Nader have no sense of humor. A crew member for *Da Ali G Show* once told *The New York Times* that "the goal is: Don't let the guest laugh, and don't get him to walk." The former generally proved much easier than the latter.

Former presidential press secretary Marlin Fitzwater cut his interview short when Ali G asked whether or not Hillary Clinton drank "from the fairy cup." "This interview is over," he announced. "Let's cut. The guy is an idiot," and stormed off. Later he said, "I'd never been

---

*Speaking of bastards . . . Gingrich later admitted he was involved in a long-term extramarital affair while trying to get President Clinton impeached for getting orally compensated by Monica Lewinsky.

lied to like that. I was two steps away from calling the sheriff."

Donald Trump also stopped his interview after Ali G pitched him an idea of manufacturing a glove to be worn while eating ice-cream cones. "I thought he was seriously retarded," Trump says. "It was a total con job. But my daughter Ivanka saw it and thought it was very cool."

During the second episode, titled "War," Ali presides over a roundtable discussion on religion. The panelists sound suspiciously like the lead-up to a joke, as they included a rabbi, an academic, an atheist, and a priest named William Byron who bears an uncanny resemblance to Barry Fitzgerald in *Going My Way*.

Father Byron looks none too happy when Ali G says to him, "Let's talk about the Mac Daddy of the Christian faith . . . what was his name again?"

The response is: "Jesus Christ."

Then Ali G asks what day Christ was supposed to have been born on.

"We celebrate his birth on the twenty-fifth of December."

"Ain't that a coincidence he wuz born on Christmas Day?"

The priest glares. Oblivious, Ali wonders, "Iz it true Jesus woz born in a stable?"

"It's possible. There was no room in the inn."

"Well, that's coz it woz Christmas."

*(crickets)*

By comparison, perennial Green Party presidential candidate and consumer advocate Ralph Nader seemed benevolent, at least while on camera.

> Ali G:   What's the big deal about rain forests? . . . Why would anyone want to live there with the risk of monkey droppings [plopping] on your head?
>
> Nader:   First of all, the monkeys are not eager to search out these natives and plop on them.
>
> Ali G:   Anything be possible.

The two bonded enough that Nader happily performed a little rap at the end of his segment.

Once Nader's camp realized they'd been punk'd Ali G–style, a spokesman complained, "Ralph did not know what to make of the guy. Apparently he is not a rapper. He's some sort of comedian. We certainly were not aware of that when the interview was granted.

"They said they were doing an educational special and going to gear it towards children and introduce them to civic figures. There was no indication that it would be a comedy act."

Another aide threatened angrily, "It might be grounds for a lawsuit," prompting the *National Review* to comment snidely, "Who would have thought Ralph Nader took himself so seriously?"

For his part, Sacha says he finds the reactions of his

guests "weird. For that time they're in the room with me, sometimes they totally forget who they are. And they come out with a totally different side of themselves." Baron Cohen believes they try to accept Ali G so they don't seem out of touch to young people. "They're in the room with a total idiot, and yet they're seeking his approval, as if it somehow makes them cooler."

All of which delighted Dan Mazer: "It was lovely to get back to that original sense of what Ali G was all about."

When the decision was made to bring the show across the pond, some wondered if the American audience's sense of irony was developed enough to appreciate Ali G's humor. In the end, Mazer says, he and Baron Cohen were pleasantly surprised. "They were very sophisticated. They also got the satire better than the British audience."

Unfortunately, American viewers never got to see one of Ali G's more classic encounters with feminist author Naomi Wolf, best known for her treatise on the cultural and media assault on women's self-image, *The Beauty Myth*.

Like others, Wolf was lured by claims the show was for an educational series that introduced children to current affairs, and she says she forwent a family vacation to participate, prompted by a sense of "perverted evangelism."

By all accounts, Wolf handled the first volleys well enough, calmly dismissing Ali G's assertions that women were not as qualified as men.

"If you is so equal, how come even the things that you

claim you were better at than men, like cooking, you ain't? The best chefs in the world are men like Colonel Sanders and Ronald McDonald. They are like a million times better than Wendy," referring to the hamburger chain.

Wolf conceded good-naturedly that most of the world's great chefs were men and remained gracious when Ali suggested women actually have more career opportunities than men because they can get jobs as strippers, exotic dancers, and "bitches" in rap videos.

But she was visibly affronted when Ali G mentioned, "With me girlfriend Julie I do sometimes call her me bitch in the bedroom. Those words come out and she ain't got a problem wid it."

"OK . . . I am so offended I can't even tell you."

But not so offended that she didn't agree to the final rap:

> Yo, yo, don't be sexist
> I'll let you ride in my Lexus.

Wolf later admitted in *The Sunday Times* that she had been "solidly nailed" by Sacha and his band of merry pranksters:

> Like any one-night stand in which someone who seems charming turns out to be a bit sleazy, part of it was delightful and part of it slightly nasty.

> I was pissed off about the racist humor, but let it ride because Britain, in my view, is not my country and I pick my fights.

Then she found out the show was going to be broadcast on HBO and Wolf turned into a stereotype—the feminist who takes herself far too seriously. Whether prompted by indignation or embarrassment, Wolf said she had contacted HBO's lawyers to complain about being used as a straight (wo)man "for what I felt was racist humor." She also called the Ali G character racist for impersonating a black . . . which Sacha and Mazer have always stressed Ali G is not doing.

Wolf also later asserted that she had a tense exchange with the attorneys, during which she made clear she didn't "want to be part of humor about how black women are sluts.

"It leaves a nasty karma," Wolf also said. "I'm not ashamed of trying to engage with what I thought was a clueless basketball player. My interview was based on a stereotype of a black youth being stupid and ill educated. A lot of the humor is that his presumably black girlfriend loves being called a bitch and a ho. But we have a four-hundred-year history of sexual trafficking in black women and I don't want to play."

Since Julie is, in fact, white, Wolf's ~~self-righteous~~ diatribe is not only overwrought but also off-point. Her stance prompted writer Jennifer O'Connell to bemoan, "One of the common misconceptions about feminists is that they're on permanent Code Orange terror alert for the smallest hint of politically incorrect humor. Which is why it was so disappointing to see Naomi Wolf reacting like Camilla Paglia at a convention of Page 3 models* when she got the Ali G treatment in New York last year."

Dan Mazer observed sardonically that of all the public figures they'd interviewed over the years, "she is the only one to kick up a stink about it. It is funny when you consider all these conservative behemoths who we encountered but were good-humored about it."

"She appeared to be having a great time and playing along," Sacha added.

When *New York Times* reporter Virginia Heffernen informed him that Wolf later said she had seen through the ruse, claiming she could tell Ali G's accent was fake, Sacha responded with what seemed to be genuine surprise. "What? . . . If she did see through it, why did she stay? Why would she do a rap at the end?"

As usual, Ali G would get the last words in. Asked in a June 2003 interview with *Spin.com* who had come closest to kicking his ass, he gave the honor to Wolf, whom he jokingly called "the world's most famous lezza." (In fact, she's

---

*Since 1970, *The Sun* newspaper in London has published daily topless shots of nubile females on its Page 3. Only "natural" women need apply—models with breast implants are supposedly not allowed. You be the judge: www.page3.com.

married with kids.) "She didn't come close to kickin' me ass, but she did come close to lickin' it, a'ight."

He also told *High Times,* "Dis woman called Naomi Wolf who is one of de world's leadin' feminists . . . or as we call dem in England: *lezzas.* She woz very cooperative—me can't go into pacifics but let's just say she weren't actin very lesbianically by de end."

And by the end of the snipe-fest, HBO chose not to air the interview in America. Wolf intimated that she got it yanked after threatening legal action but was vague as to a legal basis for any such lawsuit. HBO denied her complaints had any influence, stating the "decision to not use the Naomi Wolf piece was made prior to her phone call to HBO." The cable channel's official stance was that the interview had been nixed because there was no place to put it, because Sacha shot much more material than was available in the six episodes.

But Wolf wasn't the only one playing the racist card. *The New York Times* quoted black British writer Zina Saro-Wiwa's accusation that Ali G had "hijacked" black culture: "He's not casting aspersions as to what it is and isn't to act black. In his act, it is a given: People in Britain associate being 'black' with acting like an ignorant gangster. If you don't fall into this stereotype, you are considered inauthentic."

Author Marian Salzman dismissed the characterization as shortsighted. "He offends everyone [with] equal opportunity. So as a consequence he offends no one. He's a voice against political correctness at a time when we're on PC overload."

Mazer stresses that the point of the show is the guests' reactions, not Ali G's assertions:

> If anything, he exposes racism. The people who assume he's something he isn't [show] their inherent racism. He criticizes that part of the middle class who try to be something they're not.
>
> On the streets of London, you see hundreds of middle-class nice boys desperate to be Dr. Dre. It's a worldwide phenomenon, the non-black person trying to act wigger.*

Sacha agreed to limited publicity prior to the series premiere—but again, only as Ali G. Television critics hoping for a glimpse into the man behind the act were either left frustrated or charmed, depending on whether or not they thought *Da Ali G Show* was brilliant satire or been-there, done-that lowbrow gotcha humor that had been around since Allen Funt first turned his candid camera on unsuspecting civilians. Worse, Sacha's answer began to have a déjà vu quality because regardless of how

---

*Wigger: word used to describe white youth who adopt affectations of hip-hop and/or gang culture. The word is a morpheme of "white" and "nigger" and—no surprise here—is often used in a derogatory manner. Many consider the word offensive because (1) it stereotypes urban blacks and (2) it *is* offensive.

clever Baron Cohen is, Ali G by definition is limited in his scope.

To *Newsweek:* "Me hopes my new show will increase understanding between the peoples, lead to world peace and also give me da opportunity to have a one-off with a couple of fly Playboy Mansion bitches dat is way out of my league."

To *The Times:* "De real purpose of de show iz to make me homies in America tink 'bout deep tings, to bring politics to young people, but most importantly to get me famous enuf so dat me can bone bitches dat is way out of me league, a'ight."

When asked if his comedy was offensive, Sacha knew U.S. sensibilities well enough to let Ali G at least address the issue. "I ain't makin' fun of no one," he promised. "I'm just bein' me, keeping people laughing."

Not everyone found his irreverence amusing. *Washington Post* critic Tom Shales was offended by both *Da Ali G Show*'s content and the subtext: "One problem is that sometimes Cohen seems less interested in attacking funny bones than in appealing to sadistic streaks." Shales was deeply offended by Ali G's reference to the World Trade Center: "There's been enough sadness since the terrible events of 7/11." Shales said, "[Baron] Cohen is in character as the clueless Caucasian hip-hop interviewer Ali G, but nothing excuses joking about Sept. 11, 2001. The word 'tasteless' doesn't begin to cover it."

Shales also singled out a Borat segment featuring a dinner

party with members of the Sons of the American Legion, filled with "snidely smutty dinner-table conversation about porno, prostitutes, and flatulence. Is this all in fun, or is Cohen treating his victims with contempt, laughing inside about having tricked them into looking foolish on television?"

Noting that HBO had only signed *Da Ali G Show* to an initial six-episode run, Shales questioned if it would be enough time for Sacha to find an audience. "Whether Cohen can become a sensation in six weeks is problematic, but at least his heart's in the right place—most of the time, anyway, and assuming he really has one."

Tim Goodman of the *San Francisco Chronicle* lamented, "Too bad the results seem so childishly undeveloped, as Baron Cohen seems content to make everything a sex or scatological joke. You have to wonder—out loud, sometimes—whether HBO really thinks this is a quality addition to the lineup or rather something from the *Real Sex* school of programming where you don't have to be too proud of it but, damn, the people love it. . . ."

For as cool as he was toward Ali G, Goodman was positively dismissive of Borat and Bruno. "Two lesser Baron Cohen characters are Borat, a TV reporter from Kazakhstan, and Bruno, an Austrian fashion reporter. These two suffer from lack of depth and one-note jokes that the American audience has seen in a number of guises and done far better by Andy Kaufman and Mike Myers, to name just two."

In the end, Goodman found Ali G's shtick "tiring and, let's face it, needlessly cruel."

On the other hand, *The Boston Globe*'s Matthew Gilbert accused Baron Cohen of playing it safe. "He resists making real points about America, falling back on the more small-minded fun of saying dirty words in front of unsuspecting people or watching them writhe when they hear his sex talk. Ultimately, he's a version of Howard Stern's interviewer Stuttering John, only in more exotic drag."

Throughout the journalistic dissection, HBO remained bullish on Ali G. Nancy Geller, the executive responsible for acquiring the series, shrugged off the tepid reviews. "People just like good shows, and that's what this is—a good comedy show. People appreciate the British way of doing comedy."

And many critics agreed with her. "The funniest thing about the show is that people think he's legit," said Linda Stasi of the *New York Post,* saying Ali G was "as funny as TV gets." *The New York Times* agreed, deeming the series "irresistibly, corrosively funny . . . Ali G is clever, satirical and entirely free of any redeeming sentimentality."

The series premiered February 21, 2003, airing after HBO's other edgy newcomer, *Real Time with Bill Maher*. It attracted a devoted but relatively small following—as well as ongoing criticism for its purported racist content, prompting HBO's senior VP Quentin Schaffer to comment, "Through his alter egos, he delivers an obvious satire that exposes people's ignorance and prejudice in much the same way *All in the Family* did years ago."

Perhaps the difference is that it was clear to most people that Carroll O'Connor was simply an actor playing a role. But the line between fiction and reality was far more blurred with Baron Cohen.

# 9

# Ich Don't Think So . . .

**HOMOPHOBIA** is one of **THE LAST** forms OF **prejudice** that is REALLY **tolerated.**
—Sacha **BARON** Cohen

**WHILE** Sacha became the center of public attention, garnering fame and celebrity, the other man directly responsible for Ali G's success stayed firmly rooted in the background. The irony is so deep as to be a cliché—the reluctant star who shuns the spotlight and the overlooked creative partner who'll comfortably (eagerly?) tell his life knowing his privacy will remain intact. Although Mazer's dream in college was to be a stand-up comic, he seems content to work in Baron Cohen's shadow.

"Sacha is such an overwhelming force," he says, "you're always second, always invisible."

Although they hung out in college, they never performed together. Mazer was deeply involved in comedy while, he says, Sacha "had loftier goals at that point."

Mazer's own lofty goal of becoming a lawyer, along with his study habits, evaporated once he got into college. He owns up to being a poor student with little interest in attending classes or applying himself to his studies. He

"I wanted to be like John Coltrane. I hated jazz, but thought [it] would bring me a hue of sophistication and bohemianism."

spent three years at Cambridge and admits, "between my exams in my second year and my exams in my third year, I did not write a single paper.

"I did this thing called Footlights, which is the equivalent of Hasty Pudding at Harvard. . . . I spent all my time doing that, as opposed to my law degree."

He admits he probably shouldn't ever have been accepted in the first place. He did poorly on his entrance exam but told the interviewer that he wanted to play Hamlet. "He said that as a young man he too wished to play Hamlet. We bonded over the young Danish prince, and we didn't talk about law at all. If we had talked about law for even a second, he would have uncovered me as a fraud and never given me a chance."

Especially since he based his decision to study law on his enjoyment of the series *L.A. Law*. Mazer imagined himself a young Harry Hamlin, "having sex with girls on photocopiers and things like that. As soon as I got to Cambridge I realized [law] was the driest, most arid thing in history. I realized what I really was interested in was television."

Mazer found Cambridge a world unto itself and an often uncomfortable throwback to a less enlightened era. "Before we sat down to eat every day we had to sing Latin grace, and we had women who came in to make our beds every morning, called bedders."

He remembers his bedder refusing to make the bed of a fellow student after discovering he was gay, "for fear of catching AIDS. It was literally like stepping back into medieval times. Everybody else there was so incredibly square, you just had to drop a candy wrapper on the sidewalk and you'd be deemed a dangerous rebel."

Rather than abandoning his major, Mazer slogged through, because, he says, "it sounds so impressive. I can produce crass, vulgar, lowest-common-denominator TV, but it will give it a patina of credibility when I just mention I did law at Cambridge. So it's kind of a get-out-of-jail-free card for all my subsequent filth."

Instead of forging a career in stand-up, Mazer ended up writing for television. Once he reunited with Sacha, they fell into an easy collaboration. "We've spent the past five years together," Mazer told writer Jane Fryer in April 2003. "We know everything about each other—moods, favorite foods, what we will order in a restaurant when we're tired. It's more like a marriage than my relationship with Daisy.*" One topic they avoided discussing was

*Mazer met Daisy Donovan when they worked together on *The 11 O'Clock Show*. They were married in 2005 in Morocco.

money. "It's difficult and horrible because we were friends first, so we get our agents to talk about all that stuff." Mazer also noted that he and Sacha "never talk about the future."

It's obvious that Mazer is protective of Sacha and fielded answers to the questions his friend had up to then studiously avoided addressing himself. Mazer acknowledged that the decision to stay in character with the media and in personal appearances wasn't solely a creative endeavor, as had been suggested in the past.

"He's uncomfortable talking about himself and worries about what people might ask him," Mazer revealed. "Being famous has taken the edge off him. He's incredibly charismatic and when he's not working is still a brilliant laugh, but he used to always be at the center of it all." But he observed that fame had changed Sacha. "Now he's much quieter. . . . There's pressure to be funny and he worries about not being funny enough."

His discomfort with being under the microscope extends to his family, who are equally tight-lipped. "It's a remarkable story," Sacha's father, Gerald, acknowledged in the *Daily Mail,* "but I don't talk about my son's career and he doesn't talk about mine."

That didn't stop one of Gerald's employees from speaking in confidence. "He is proud of [Sacha] because he is a bright lad, and he doesn't begrudge his fame, but I think he finds it a bit hard to deal with and he considers his Ali G character rather rude and risqué.

"Gerald is shy and prefers to take a backseat. Both he and his brother are ultimately down-to-earth Welsh folk and very much see themselves as being from Cardiff. They have not forgotten their roots at all. As for the character Ali G, I can't help but feel that it might have a lot more to do with the family's roots than one might expect."

Toss Bruno and Borat into the mix and that's a highly intriguing suggestion.

Each episode of the American series was broken down into vignettes. In addition to Ali G, there were two other segments: "Borat's Guide to the U.S." and "Funkyzeit mit Bruno" (Funkytime with Bruno). Borat appeared in every episode while Bruno appeared in all but two.

During filming, Borat and Bruno engendered the strongest reactions and responses from people. "You'd think Ali G would wind people up more," Mazer muses, "but because he's an intimidating character in his own right, people lay off him. Because Bruno is a

Bruno's theme song is "Crank It Up" by Scooter, from the album *Our Happy Hardcore*.

camp character and Borat is an idiot, they think they can bully them."

Another difference between the characters is that while Borat is an ignorant, albeit good-natured, racist, Bruno is a walking target. So Sacha felt it was not inappropriate portraying a gay man. "I think it would be different if Bruno was coming out with very homophobic or gay stereotypes," Baron Cohen explains. "But he's not. He's the subject of a lot of homophobia . . . it's a lot more dangerous."

When Bruno made his debut in 1998 on Britain's Paramount Comedy Channel, he had plastered-down hair and a mustache and was dressed down in sensible slacks, an open-collared shirt, and a leather driving jacket.

Under Alper's guidance, Bruno became less seventies Eurotrash and more new-millennium Amsterdam gay district with a blond Mohawk, sleeveless vests, and formfitting pants. Bruno is as careful with his personal grooming as he is with his fashion sense.

Compared to his other characters, "Bruno is the most pristine of all of them," Sacha says. "Hygiene is incredibly important; I shave fully."

"Obviously it is the camp way to be entirely hairless," Mazer adds. "There was a debate how much to get waxed."

For the record, Baron Cohen says he doesn't shave his chest but admits he does "coiffure my bush. But that's as far as I'll go."

Bruno, who calls himself the voice of Austrian youth, is

a correspondent for *OJRF—Österreichischer Jungen Rundfunk* (Austrian Boy Broadcast). Fashion is his beat, celebrities are his targets, and homosexuality is his favorite topic, which he pursues with guileless enthusiasm. Bruno isn't just camp but blithely gay.

In his interview with Lance Quinn, a Little Rock, Arkansas, pastor whose life's mission is to convert gays into heterosexuals, Bruno confessed he may have tendencies . . . lots and lots of tendencies, and asked for clarification on what exactly is acceptable, nonhomosexual behavior:

Bruno:   Showering with a friend?

Quinn:   That's forbidden by God's word.

Bruno:   Watching *Will & Grace*?

Quinn:   It's ungodly.

Bruno:   Being fabulous?

Quinn:   First Corinthians VI says that's an effeminate lifestyle.

Bruno:   Eating brunch?

Quinn:   If you're eating brunch with Christian friends and there's no one else around who's going to seduce you into sin, it's OK.

Whereas Ali G produced cringe-worthy moments because of his cluelessness, watching Bruno is frequently nerve-wracking. It's one thing to set yourself up for ridicule, anger, or insult, quite another to put your personal safety on

the line. Bruno's segments that take place in urban areas
such as New York, Miami, or Los Angeles tended to concentrate on celebrities and fashion. The tone may have been
bitchy, the exchanges dishy, but there was little, if any, in-
tolerance displayed. To many people in the entertainment
and fashion industries, being gay is simply not an issue given
much thought.

Yes, partly because so many are gay themselves, but
also because artists in any creative field have historically
been more accepting of lifestyles that veer off the mainstream path. In fact, some would argue a chicken-or-egg
conundrum: Are they gay because they are innately creative or are they creative because they are gay? In the
way a certain type of male baldness is associated with an
overabundance of body hair, could gays be genetically
predisposed to the arts? Or are they drawn to the arts
because that field inherently allows for freedom of ex-
pression?

Conversely, what is it about so many red-state young
men, particularly in the South, that they not just condone
but incite and encourage blatant bigotry and violence?
Sacha and Mazer made no effort to explain such long-
standing cultural conflicts, but they did use homophobia as
a backdrop for comedic effect when they ventured below
the Mason-Dixon Line.

In Daytona Beach for spring break, a group of exuberant college boys agree to be filmed giving a party cheer.
Bruno faces the camera and shouts, "Hello, and welcome

Playing Bruno
frequently
put Sacha in
harm's way.

from Daytona Beach, where all the great boys in America come to be gay!"

He punches his fist in the air on the word "gay" and a couple of the young men gamely follow along and hoot, although most look at each other hesitantly.

Out of the pack, you hear one of them ask: "Wait . . . 'gay' means 'happy,' right?"

Bruno turns and says matter-of-factly, "No—gay sex."

Fade to Bruno befriending five members of a wrestling team hanging on the beach in their motor home. He gets one of the guys to show him some wrestling moves and later they accommodate his request to show their asses while flexing their muscles. Bruno calls Jim over and asks if he'll give a shout out to his television audience. At his prompting, Jim enthusiastically repeats the lines Bruno feeds him:

"Hello! . . . This is Jim. . . . And I'm saying hi . . . from Daytona Beach, Florida! . . . to Austrian . . . Gay TV!"

Jim does an abrupt double take. "Huh? Austrian Gay TV? Get the fuck out of here!" He walks in an agitated circle, then comes back. "You say Gay TV? Get the fuck out of here! No, no, there's no fucking Gay TV involved in this!"

Sacha later told Conan O'Brien that his cameraman got punched out by one of the wrestlers before they managed to pack up and leave. Mazer says most of the time they've been able to get away without bloodshed and they can "make a thirty-second exit from anywhere with camera crews and lights. It's like *Charlie's Angels*."

As they got farther into the heart of Dixie, Bruno trod on more toes. In the "Belief" episode, Bruno begins his report standing in front of a "Pawn & Guns" sign. "I've come to the gayest part of America—Alabama!"

Cut to Bruno at the Alabama–Mississippi college football game where he incurred the wrath of the drunken fans. Sacha remembers how "sixty thousand people in the stands started chanting 'faggot,' and started throwing stuff at me, taunting me and spitting at me and threatening to kill me. And those kinds of situations are a lot more common when you're playing a gay character."

Rather than turn off the cameras and get out of Dodge, Baron Cohen was more excited than nervous, so he remained in character. He found that assuming the role of a gay man "taunting sixty thousand bigots [was] very invigorating." Sacha says the only way he got out unharmed "was by switching clothes with the sound man." Ironically, suspecting the situation might turn ugly, Sacha had hired a bodyguard to accompany him that day. "The moment the crowd started jeering and booing and chanting 'faggot,' I turned to see where the bodyguard was and I saw the back of his head as he was running out of the stadium, so he left us high and dry."

Sacha later returned to interview running back Shaud Williams, who calmly explained to Bruno that he wasn't gay when asked what he wanted to say to all the men in Austria wanting to date him. That exchange was in stark contrast to Bruno's encounter with the organizer of the Pro-America Expo. Their chat starts out amicable enough, with the organizer explaining that freedom means not having the government looking over his shoulder.

Bruno responds by saying in Austria freedom means he and his boyfriend Diesel can walk down the street holding hands without anybody staring at them. "Is that the kind of freedom you are campaigning for?"

"I'm not too hot on your right to hold hands with your boyfriend," the organizer tells him, "but what you do in the privacy of your own home, as long as you stay away from my kids . . ."

Bruno proceeds to tell the man how attractive he is and asks if he's bisexual.

"I'm not bi and I'm not gay and if you're going to speak on that subject, you can take a hike." The man's slight smile turns grim. "You're not my type."

Bruno is taken aback, stung. "Is it because I'm too fat?"

The man abruptly ends the interview and leans forward with menacing intensity. "You want to be professional, be a professional; don't be some fucking fag!"

It's as close to a verbal lynching as viewers are likely to see on television. In another episode, at a gun show in Arkansas Bruno pressed his luck by flirting with a barrel-chested attendee named Daniel. After Daniel tells Bruno he doesn't know anything about gay people, doesn't know any gay people, and is not gay himself, Bruno looks perplexed and asks why he's denying it.

"If you call me gay one more time, I'm fixing to knock every tooth outta your head, you understand what I'm sayin'? 'Cause I've done told you that I'm not gay. . . . Be careful what you say . . . be real careful what you say."

But no matter how tense the situation, Baron Cohen believes it's imperative to remain in character. "That's something I'm quite rigorous about, from the moment they meet me until the moment I leave. . . . We didn't ever want to have that 'Hey, gotcha' moment, and they go, 'Ah, right, it was a joke,' because we want it to be a real experience."

The production's final stop for filming was in Georgia, where they attended a neo-Nazi white supremacist rally. Instead of wearing the traditional robes and hoods of the Klan, members of the group wore Arab-esque headwear. Bruno thinks the look is fabulous and asks the leader how they all get their skin so white. "Do you use moisturizer?"

It went downhill from there.

"I can't remember what the trigger question was, but all of a sudden the guy we were interviewing exploded," Mazer recalls. "He started physically attacking the cameraman and reaching for his gun. We legged it like no one's ever legged it.

"In the meantime, two guys dressed as Arab sheiks got wind of it and started yelling at us. As we're driving away, we see the main Nazi guy chasing us followed by his coterie of Arab sheik Nazis, all shaking their fists. It was like a scene at the end of *Scooby-Doo*."

Where Bruno was a lightning rod for barefaced bigotry, the third character in Sacha's coterie, Borat, revealed a more insidious strain: a latent racism simmering beneath the surface of American civility.

"So, are there any skinheads who aren't gay?" isn't the best icebreaker in Georgia.

# 10

# The Man from Kazakhstan

The **CHARACTER** of the **IDIOT** is always funny. That's a **CHARACTER** that can **BE** amusing **TO** **PEOPLE** in many cultures.
—Sacha **BARON** Cohen

**THE** basic premise of Borat Sagdiyev is that he's a fish out of water trying to put his surroundings into a context he understands. A cultural tabula rasa.* As a result, Borat becomes the perfect mirror on the wall, although in this case it's the reflection that frequently comes up cracked and flawed.

By the time *Da Ali G Show* came to America, Borat had undergone a subtle but distinct development from Alexi Krickler from Moldova and even from early Borat appearances on Ali G's British series. In those, the focus was on his cluelessness, such as when he interviewed a rugby player from the British Lions and spent painful minutes believing they actually had lions playing the game.

While still vacuous, the focus of the humor shifted. His struggle to grasp cultural concepts remained the same, but for "Borat's Guide to the U.S." his prejudices hovered

---

*Tabula rasa: in philosophy, the unformed, featureless mind; literal translation of Latin is "a blank slate."

closer to the surface. What makes the humor so dark and the satire so rich is that on a very basic level Borat is likeable, gregarious, earnest—a man-child. So the offensiveness of his deep anti-Semitism and dismissive misogyny is softened and comes across as less dangerous than it is. More to the point, it invites confidences and lures others to reveal their own dark corners.

"Borat essentially works as a tool," Sacha explains. "By himself being anti-Semitic, he lets people lower their guard and expose their own prejudice, whether it's anti-Semitism or an acceptance of anti-Semitism."

His hygiene was also noticeably worse. Sacha bought Borat's gray nylon suit back around 1998 for thirty dollars and says, "I have never washed it since I got it . . . and it totally stinks."

Mazer clarifies: "It stinks beyond human imagination. It's the most disgusting thing you can imagine. When Sacha is Borat, he never washes the night before an interview so *he's* a little bit stinky." Nor does Borat use deodorant.

So, Baron Cohen says with worrisome glee, whenever he enters a room, "there's immediately this terrible . . . dreadful Soviet Bloc smell the moment I walk in." Sacrificing personal hygiene is simply part of creating a believable character. "The smell is an added thing for people to believe that I'm from a country where hygiene isn't a necessity." But Baron Cohen admits that staying in character creates "a lot of tension during the day."

As Borat, Baron Cohen says, "I don't change my underpants." Definitely too much info. . . .

Even the underpants are authentic and provided by his father. "Yeah . . . That was my dad's underpants, which are made by the Norwegian navy."

So it follows that the bushy hair and mustache are Sacha's as well, which made shooting the segments for the HBO series a juggling act.

"The whole schedule of the show is literally governed by my facial hair and how fast I can grow a beard," he acknowledges. "We can't do one day Borat and the next day Ali G. We kind of do Borat for a block and then on to Ali G."

Andrew Newman, who produced the first *Da Ali G Show* series, says it is Sacha's ability to immerse himself so completely without regard for his own comfort, ego, or self-esteem that enables him to pull off his comic scams so successfully. "He is a funny actor, but more than that he becomes the characters he's playing, certainly with . . . Borat. He sort of has a mix of Peter Sellers's acting and a

Hull came to bitterly resent Emu's popularity.

Rod Hull* sort of bottle.† He can just look someone in the eye and say, 'Is it coz I'ze black?' even though he is quite obviously not Ali G and he is quite obviously not black. He has a psychotic ability to play these characters. . . . He is able to mix things on a different level. He is able to be at once clever and very stupid."

Perhaps the most surprising thing, Newman says, is that out of character Sacha "is surprisingly normal, a warm-hearted guy."

And Baron Cohen wants people to think the same of Borat. As Ali G, Sacha would begin each interview asking relatively straightforward questions to get them comfortable with the notion of being interviewed by this delusional

---

*For those of you who can't remember, Rod Hull was a popular British entertainer in the 1970s and '80s. His sidekick was Emu, an overly aggressive arm puppet who would pester anyone, regardless of rank or privilege. Although Emu was mute, his personality usually overshadowed Hull's. Hull died in 1999 after falling off the roof of his house while trying to fix the antenna.

†Bottle: nerve; derived from cockney slang, where "bottle" referred to "arse." So losing one's bottle meant losing the contents of one's bowels. Charming, eh?

gangsta wannabe. Once their guard was down, he'd go for the comedic kill.

Baron Cohen's process with Borat was geared to gauge his subject's susceptibility. It usually started with a gift. For example, he handed Alan Keyes, a black, far right-wing political activist, what he identified as the rib of a Jew.

Keyes accepted the rib and thanked Borat—until he realized the cameras were rolling. He ripped off his microphone and headed out. He was eventually cajoled back after the production staff convinced him it had been a misunderstanding: Borat had actually said "dew's rib." Mollified, Keyes stayed.

The crew helps promote the ruse. "What we do is pretend that we are a London film crew who have been landed with him on that morning," Mazer says. "We plead ignorance. We tell them not to blame us; we just apologize."

The biggest problem was figuring out what *not* to include in each segment. For every segment, which ran approximately five minutes, hours of footage had been shot. "There is so much footage that we love but we know we must lose," Mazer acknowledges. "We hope to be able to use some of the unseen footage on E4* or on an extra DVD."

Those being interviewed were told Borat Sagdiyev was a well-known journalist from Kazakhstan's state-run television

---

*The digital companion of Channel 4, aimed at 16 to 35 year olds.

network. Mazer says, "We chose a country such as Kazakhstan as we were confident that there was little chance of
meeting anyone who knew anything about it." Their closest
call happened in England. "Sacha . . . was getting a group of
English rugby players to sing songs for him in Cambridge.
They then asked him to sing a Kazakhstani song; he was
floundering but then basically repeated the same word about
fifty times to some made-up tune. I think he got away with it
as they were so pissed."

Now that digital technology, cable, satellite, and the In-
ternet have shrunk the world—and due to the increased
need for programming as television censorship in many
countries has reduced in recent years—the idea that a reporter from Kazakhstan would be in America doing a series
of shows about life in the United States was hardly far-
fetched. With so many countries hating the US just on principle for having too much—too much industry, too much
food, too much money, too much arrogance, too much
oil—most Americans are willing to accommodate a foreign
visitor in hopes of changing that perception, at least on an
individual level. Sacha took advantage of that generosity of
spirit and used it to expose their foibles and, in some cases,
their demons, such as couching anti-Semitism within the
context of devout faith.

During an interview with Borat, James Broadwater, an
evangelical Christian who was a Republican congressional
candidate from Mississippi at the time of his interview, announced that the only way to Heaven was through Jesus.

When Borat asked what that meant for non-Christians, such as Jews, Broadwater said, "I would have to say, they go to Hell."

The candidate later defended his comment, claiming he was told that the interview was for a show about the American political system that would only be broadcast in foreign countries. He also reiterated that "anyone who accepts Jesus Christ as Lord and Savior will spend eternity in Heaven, while everyone who rejects him will spend eternity in Hell." Broadwater added that "the liberal, anti-God media needs to be brought under the strict control of the FCC—and that as soon as possible."

By the way—Broadwater lost the election, apparently too extreme even for Mississippi.

When asked if it was more fun punking Brits or Americans, Sacha said it depended on the class. "The best targets— the legitimate targets—are successful, powerful white men, who rule the country. And in Britain the upper class are incredibly accommodating. You can punch someone from the upper class in the face, and they'll go, 'Oh, I'm dreadfully sorry.' They'll never ever throw you out of the room."

Americans are edgier and more blunt and quicker to say, "All right, enough is enough." Case in point: Andy Rooney. Sacha says it was clear Rooney disliked Ali G the moment he came into the room. "He started asking: 'Have you done this before? Is English your first language?' And then basically tries to stop the interview after one question."

Mazer feels Americans are both more polite and more volatile. "In England the people we interviewed are slower burners; you can start things off slow, go harder for laughs, and then slow it down again. The people we interviewed [in the United States] were more polite, but only up to a point. If we pushed them too hard then they could suddenly become furious, at times violently angry." He recalls being in Arizona where "they had this cage built to channel the music of angels and Borat was in it simulating a sexual act. The chap went mad and actually called the police."

That was just one of several encounters with law enforcement for Borat. He never got arrested, but he told Howard Stern his film was once confiscated. It happened during a segment with a "healer" who was trying to massage an unyieldingly tense Borat. The healer left the room for a few moments to give Borat time to relax. He came back to find Borat (apparently) masturbating with gusto. The healer ended up calling the police. Sacha said the cops let him go but took the film, which was never returned.

But, Mazer says, by and large, Baron Cohen thrives on such moments. "He has no fear. The more nerve-wracking the situation, the more brilliant he is. Sacha sometimes is quiet and maybe has a few nerves in the car on the way to an interview, but when he is in character and actually becomes Borat, then he is 'in the zone.' I think he thinks he actually has become Borat."

Sacha explains it's essential "to get people to feel relaxed enough that they fully open up. And they say things that they never would on normal TV. So if they are anti-Semitic or racist or sexist, they'll say it." Philosophically, he believes one function of documentary filmmaking is to make people so comfortable, they forget the camera is there. That's when "they would really say their true feelings. And here was a way, by creating a foreign character, to get them to genuinely explain what they feel about particular subjects—but immediately. You wouldn't have to leave the camera in the room for three months before they'd start opening up."

That he was an idiot was even better. "By having someone who's a little backward—who doesn't know how to flush a toilet or how to cross a road, anything that we take for granted in Western society—you've got this wonderful mechanism *of allowing people* to really explain what their values are or how society functions in the West."

Baron Cohen recounts the time Borat was visiting a private gentlemen's club in Mississippi that had an all-black serving staff:

> There's this unsaid racism; there's still segregation there. I can't remember the actual line, but I asked if he had slaves, and he said, "Slavery's over now. . . . It's good."
>
> And I go, "Good for them!" He goes, "Yeah, good for them. Bad for us."
>
> That guy normally would never say that he thought it's a shame that slavery doesn't exist

anymore. But because he's in the room with somebody who's totally naive and seems to not mind that slavery existed, he was fully honest.

During the first series, "Borat's Guide" covered dating, etiquette, being a real man, acting, baseball, and the South. One of Mazer's favorite bits in the show came during the final episode of the first season when Borat shows a woman at a rodeo naked pictures of his wife.

They came up with the idea at one of their brainstorming sessions. "We said to a researcher: 'Find us a nude model to pose to be Borat's wife,'" Mazer recalls. "He bought a seedy porno catalogue and finally brought this woman into the offices."

They went down to the basement, which had a couch. The researcher couldn't bring himself to take the photos, so Mazer says Jason Alper did the deed. "At one point he asked her to pose in the 'flying V' position . . . something we had never heard of."

With the genitals-baring, gynecologically explicit Polaroids in hand, Mazer says, "we just had to make sure we got the moment right to use them. A number of times I could see Sacha, as Borat, ready to get the photos out to show someone, but the time wasn't quite right."

It finally was at the Llano County rodeo in Texas, where Borat is sitting in the stands next to a young, blond Dallas Cheerleader–type Texas beauty who's holding her dachshund.

"I have a wife," Borat tells her. "Do you want to see her picture?"

"Yes."

He gets a set of Polaroids out from his jacket pocket. The top picture is of a matronly woman dressed modestly in a sweater.

The woman is duly complimentary. "Oh, she's pretty. She couldn't come with you . . . ?" Her voice trails off as she flips through the photos. "Did you know that picture was in there?" she asks, more surprised than offended, revealing a photo of an overweight naked middle-aged woman with her legs spread wide apart.

"Yes," Borat answers, confused. "That is my wife."

The young woman laughs heartily and smacks Borat on the leg. "That's more of your wife than *I* wanted to see!"

Amazingly, Borat engendered as much good will as Bruno provoked loathing. "Despite him holding these terrible opinions, people really like him," Sacha says. "For example, in Mississippi at the wine tasting, I was going, 'Do you live in a house?'

"And he said, 'Yeah, you can come and stay with me tonight.' They totally loved me, those guys. I kissed one of them on the lips . . . because I was so drunk at that point."

Needing to stay in character, he couldn't admit he was a drinking lightweight. "I'm not a big drinker at the best of times. I'm almost a teetotaler." But that night, "I think I downed about twenty-one or twenty-two glasses of wine in an hour to try and convince them." He then excused himself to go to the bathroom, where he "totally passed out, and they all came in. My director was really scared that I'd wake up and go [in normal British accent], 'Allo! What's going on here? Allo . . . ,' that I'd come up as Sacha Baron Cohen. But luckily I opened my eyes and went, 'I want more wine!'

"I woke up in character!"

What's surreal to consider is that none of the people he encounters know they are going to be on prime-time television until the episode airs, even though they do sign release forms. More fascinating is that no "civilian" ever lodged a complaint to HBO. When asked if he thinks there's a sense of betrayal, he dismisses the notion. "I think most people don't," Sacha says. "I think ninety-nine percent don't."

At the same time, he refrains from calling his American dupes good sports. "I think the term 'sports' is wrong because that implies that they are playing along and they realize they're part of the game. As far as I've seen, they're not."

Although he has no idea how many people ultimately know they've appeared on his HBO show, he assumes, "A lot of them hear about it. . . . A lot of them hear about it through their kids, who call them up and go, 'Dad, you're on TV. You're on *Da Ali G Show.*' They suddenly achieve this kind of street cred."

Indeed, when contacted after the series aired, two of those duped were good-naturedly amused. During the "Acting" episode, shot in New York, Borat developed a crush on actress Jennifer DiFrancesco and tried, unsuccessfully, to get her to go out with him.

She says she first found out who Borat really was when a friend called her at one in the morning and said, "I just spit out my Chinese food. You're on TV." That's when I knew."

When she mentioned it to other friends later, "They were like, 'You haven't heard of Ali G? I love that show.' But I haven't owned a television in about eight years."

DiFrancesco says she got involved in the shoot when her acting teacher "asked if anyone could come in and do some improv and I thought it would be good for me to do because I've never been in front of a camera before. I figured, no one will see this and it would be a good little exercise of courage. I'm not a professional by any means. At the time of taping, I had taken about seven classes or so."

Even though Borat was hitting on her, she wasn't offended. "I knew he was just trying to be funny."

Randall Shelley, who played in the baseball game Borat attended, agreed to a friendly post-game wrestling match in the locker room, which made it to air.

"We had lost our game that day horribly. The other team, who were an affiliate of the Boston Red Sox, had beat us by at least ten runs. Our coach told us, 'Some guy wants to interview you all; just be courteous and answer his questions; he bought you all dinner.' So we were thinking, *Cool—free food.*"

Shelley says he never suspected it was a hoax. "After the

game I called my wife and parents and told them the story of an interesting guy named Borat who came in our clubhouse and interviewed us. For me at the time it was just a crazy story about a crazy man who didn't act normal. Sacha never comes out of character the entire time, so there was no reason to not believe that he was a fake."

After the season ended, Shelley was talking to a friend about a British show called *Da Ali G* and his favorite character on it, Borat. "I said, 'Did you just say Borat?' " And then I realized that it all had been a fake and I was wondering why I didn't sign any waivers for me to appear on his show. . . . I realized sooner or later it would be on TV."

Sometimes, though, the camaraderie was chilling. On Howard Stern's radio show, Baron Cohen described an incident that never made it to air in the United States.

"I'm interviewing this guy [Gordon] in Texas on this ranch," Sacha recalled. "It's basically like this exotic zoo. But instead of just looking at the animals, you can shoot them as well." Borat and Gordon commiserate with each other over Jews, with Gordon explaining that the Nazis had to solve the Jewish problem because the Jews controlled all the money in Germany.

> Borat:   It is a shame you cannot have in one of this.
> [Borat gestures at the ranch.] Deer and then a
> Jew. Then you can hunt the Jew.

Gordon:  [laughs] You can't be this way in this country!

Borat:  But why not?

Gordon:  It's OK with me. But it's not with other people.

"'They had to solve the Jewish problem,'" Sacha repeated in his interview with Howard Stern. "And he made it sound like such a perfectly reasonable thing."

Stern asked why they didn't air the interview. "Was it because of the pressure?"

The short answer was yes. "We aired that in England actually. But there were elements in HBO that thought trivializing the Holocaust—"

"But *he* was trivializing it!" Stern interrupted, even more riled than usual. "You know what this country has become in a lot of ways? Like we have to protect the stupid people. We can't let the idiots of this country watch this. . . . We're worried they won't get the joke."

But a lot of Jews weren't getting the joke, either, especially after Borat's second-season "Country Western" episode. The segment started on an amusing note when Borat interviewed country music legend Porter Wagoner, who agreed to help him write a song. Borat suggested a song about his sister, explaining she "was voted best sex in mouth . . . and second or third best prostitute."

Wagoner nods and says, "Well, that's great . . . that's a talent, too."

We next see Borat duded out in what appears to be a leather vest over shirt and tie, wearing an *Urban Cowboy* Stetson hat, singing at a country western bar in Tucson. Strumming a guitar, he serenades the crowd with "In My Country, There Is a Problem." In the first verse, he complains about how long it takes to travel around Kazakhstan. The second verse addresses another issue: Jews. He encourages everyone to sing along with the chorus: "Throw the Jew down the well . . ."

Rather than boo him off the stage or walk out, a majority of the other bar patrons obliged and started singing along. Enthusiastically. By the end of the song, the crowd is a-hootin' and a-hollerin' in apparent convivial approval. Even those who appear clearly uncomfortable stay silent and stay put.

Sacha admits he wasn't sure how to interpret their reaction. "The question is: Does it reveal anti-Semitism? Was everyone in the bar anti-Semitic?" He referred again to Ian Kershaw's belief that you only need to be indifferent. "It's that indifference that's actually quite dangerous."

The performer in Sacha, though, can't help but be intrigued. "It's fascinating to see how people are going to react. It's exciting however they react—whether they're going to answer with integrity or reveal certain prejudices that they have. . . . I didn't know the crowd was going to start chanting along or even that certain members of the audience would start miming horns."

What was offensive to many Jewish leaders was their

belief Baron Cohen was inciting anti-Semitism. After the segment aired, HBO was barraged with calls. The Anti-Defamation League, a U.S.-based Jewish rights group, complained to HBO executives, and ADL national director Abraham Foxman wrote an open letter to Baron Cohen.

"While we understand this scene was an attempt to show how easily a group of ordinary people can be encouraged to join in an anti-Semitic chorus," Foxman wrote, "we are concerned that the irony may have been lost on some of your audience or worse still that they simply accepted Borat's statements about Jews at face value . . . in attempting to expose bigotry and prejudice you also bear a responsibility to be sensitive.

"It is a very thin line between what's offensive and what's supposed to be funny and that line was crossed."

When the show aired in Britain, rabbis were more forceful and demanded Sacha end his "offensive and immoral" show. Rabbi Shaul Rosenblatt told *The Age,* "I would guess his parents are not too happy with what he is doing: it's not the kind of thing we would want a nice Jewish boy to do."

The paper quoted another rabbi suggesting that the show was offering "people with malevolent intent a further excuse to go round bashing Jews."

Baron Cohen disagrees. "I think the reason it's not really encouraging anti-Semitism is that it's showing that all forms of prejudice are really delusional. So, for example, Borat believes that Jews were behind 9/11. However, he also believes that Jews can shift their shape into insects, which is clearly delusional."

It's interesting that Dan Mazer sees it differently and admits there is a danger of reinforcing bigotry and anti-Semitism with their comedy. "When we did Ali G, the idea was to parody the racist, misogynistic, homophobic rappers." To their surprise, Ali G "became a hero to these fifteen-year-olds who repeated his views as if they were enlightening." But Mazer stresses the importance of not pandering to that. "We are making a satirical point and ignorant racists are always going to be ignorant racists who are going to latch onto what they latch onto in order to support that, but if we can enlighten a few people and be sophisticated enough to make a satirical point, then that's worth the possible negative effects."

It would not be the last time Borat was the center of an ideological storm. And the next time around, it would be on a global scale. But as the summer of 2004 approached, Baron Cohen was getting ready to give Ali G a kind of farewell tour.

# 11

# A Chapter Ends

You **IZ** da **elite**; you **WILL** be **tomorrow's CAPTAINS of industry.** Sittin' **IN FRONT** of **me** is **PROBLY DA NEXT Bill Gates,** Donald Trump . . . **OR** EVEN **Ronald McDonald.**

**—ALI G** TO **HARVARD'S** CLASS OF **2004**

**IN** November 2003, Sacha bought a spacious Victorian home in the posh Hampstead area of North London for an estimated £1 million. While the house was located in one of London's most exclusive neighborhoods, it also came with a rather notorious past. The previous owner was popular game show host Michael Barrymore. In March 2001, a meat factory worker named Stuart Lubbock was found dead, wearing only his underwear, in Barrymore's pool. The coroner determined Lubbock had a cornucopia of drugs in his system and found he had sustained severe anal injuries.

Barrymore, who had long been closeted, had finally come out in 1995—to the apparent surprise of his then wife, Cheryl, who was also his manager. The classic sticky wicket. Divorce followed. So did the his-and-hers tell-all books. A brief summary:

She:   He was a bastard.

He:   She was a control freak who drove him to drink-
        ing, drugs, and gay affairs.

Not that she was bitter or anything, but when on her deathbed in 2005—after being diagnosed with an aggressive form of lung cancer just six weeks earlier—Cheryl elicited promises that Michael not be told of her condition or be allowed to attend her funeral.

Great dish, to be sure, but I digress.

Media and public speculation that Lubbock died at one of Barrymore's alleged drug-filled gay sex parties ruined his career. ITV canceled his contract, and his new family series, *Kids Say the Funniest Things,* never aired. In 2003, he left England and moved to New Zealand, where he eventually filed for bankruptcy.*

And that's how Baron Cohen got a great house with a tragic past. Unfortunately, he didn't have a whole lot of time to spend there. As the second-season premiere of HBO's *Da Ali G Show* neared in the summer of 2004, Sacha found himself in unfamiliar territory—promoting the show not in character, but as himself.

Whether his reluctance to show the world his real self was born from a desire for privacy or a savvy marketing plan, the end result was that Sacha Baron Cohen had become an enigmatic figure. While not exactly in Howard

---

*In June 2007, Barrymore and two others were arrested on suspicion of murder. Barrymore was released on bail without charge and has strenuously maintained his innocence.

Hughes territory, he seemed to be approaching a critical point where the social messages in his comedy were being overshadowed by curiosity about the man himself, with people wondering, *What's he afraid of us seeing?*

So for the second HBO season, he adopted a new approach, kind of. Although he appeared as himself on various talk shows chatting up the second season on HBO, he only talked about the characters, never about himself. What was most telling is how much other comics clearly enjoyed Sacha.

He made his first appearance as himself on the *Late Show,* where David Letterman laughed in genuine delight when Sacha described, as Bruno, how attractive David was. When Letterman asked if Sacha had moved to L.A., a flash of discomfort passed over Baron Cohen's face and he muttered that no, he was not living there, and immediately launched into an anecdote about the foibles of being in Hollywood: "I find I keep making a lot of faux pas when I meet famous people. . . . Like I met Jim Carrey at a party and we were chatting and I said, 'Do you have a girlfriend at the moment?' And he said, 'No, I'm single.' And then this quite attractive young girl walks past and I say, 'What about her?' Then she turns to Jim Carrey and says, 'Dad, I'm just going to be over there a few minutes.' "

When Sacha first walked out on *The Daily Show,* Jon Stewart gave him the once-over and announced: "You clean up nice," then listened while Sacha explained the concept behind Ali G: "He basically asks very stupid questions to some of the most intelligent and important people in your country."

Stewart did a double take. "You know what's weird? I do that, too."

Sacha related the time he interviewed Richard Kerr, deputy director of the CIA. "So [Ali G] would ask, 'What punishment do you think they should give suicide bombers? . . . Are you worried terrorists will hijack a train and drive it into the White House?' " and had Stewart doubled over in belly laughs.

"What's frightening about that, on so many levels," Stewart said once he regained his composure, "is, he's in the CIA and when they said 'Ali G,' he didn't look you up? They don't have a database that says: 'I don't think that's a real guy'?"

When asked if there would be a third series of Ali G or was he now too well-known to pull it off, Baron Cohen said it remained to be seen.

"If you stick with our intelligence services," Stewart commented dryly, "the show could run forever."

Although the show was still considered a cult hit in the United States, Ali G had gained enough notoriety among young viewers that he, not Sacha Baron Cohen, was asked to deliver a speech at Harvard's 2004 Class Day, a traditionally lighthearted event that takes place the day before graduation. He joined such past speakers as Rodney Dangerfield,

Ali G addresses Harvard graduates. *Courtesy of Wikipedia (www.wikipedia.com)*

Walter Cronkite, Bono, and that poster girl of lightheartedness, Mother Teresa:*

Despite it being a hot day with the temperature in the nineties, Ali G showed up covered head to toe in a red tracksuit embossed with *Professor of Erbology* printed on the back of his warm-up jacket. "Normally da only public speaking I does is to twelve people," he told the crowd, "and it's, well, easy; all me has to say is me name and da words 'not guilty.'"

In his speech, Ali G applauded the diversity of the graduating class. "It's fantastic to see dat Harvard has finally let in so many women. A lot of you is probably feminists—or as we call dem in England: lezzas. I agree dat you gotta treat women with respect—it's da least dat bitches deserve."

At one point he joked: "Really regretting bringing your grandparents now, aren't you?" Then he went on to say:

---

*When Will Ferrell addressed the graduates in 2003, after making fun of Harvard he funneled a beer. Mother Teresa, we are told, did not.

"Relationships should be brought into dis, da twentieth century. You women out dere shouldn't have to do da cookin' and da cleanin' when you come home from work. You should do it before you leave in da morning."

In closing, Ali G offered these words of wisdom: "I look out and I see thousands of people wiv different hopes and different dreams, but it is important never to forget where u all came from, becuz black, white, brown, or Pakistani, we all come from de same place—da punani."

The reaction, surprisingly, was mostly positive. "I thought it was funny, but I thought he crossed the line a couple of times," graduating senior Javier Valle told *The Boston Globe*. "My mom may have squirmed a little bit."

*Globe* reporter Carolyn Y. Johnson described the scene:

> Some students clasped their hands over their mouths in both amusement and shock. It was a far cry from the eloquent student speeches. It also marked a new extreme for Harvard's roster of Class Day speakers. . . .
>
> After speaking, when Ali G returned to the stage to receive an honorary gift from the student body, a policeman accompanied him and he held his hands behind his back as if handcuffed. "Police brutality," he joked before lifting a shot glass with several members of the class of 2004 for a celebratory toast.

The fact was, Ali G's shock value paled considerably when compared to Borat. And by the time the second HBO season was in full swing, Borat had become the lightning rod figure. Ali G was just a goof who caused annoyance. . . .

Sam Donaldson did the rap Ali G had written for him:

> *News ain't just for the white men*
> *It's for the bros and sisters, too.*

Then, the nonplussed newsman looked offstage and pleaded, "What in God's name *is* this?"

But Borat got under people's skin, most notably, in the autumn of 2004, the skin of Kazakh officials. Yerzhan Ashykbayev, a senior foreign ministry official in Kazakhstan, told *The Mirror* in London that Borat's act "could be regarded as an attempt to fire up interethnic tension."

*The New Yorker* reported that Roman Vassilenko, the press attaché at the Kazakh Embassy in the United States, accused Baron Cohen of, basically, unfairly dissing Kazakhstan.*

Vassilenko was pained over the idea Kazakhs would throw a party after throwing a Jew in the well and with other Boratisms such as "in Kazakhstan we say, 'God, man, horse, dog, then woman, then rat.' "

---

*In related news, town officials in Slough, Berkshire, complained that the BBC Two comedy *The Office* had made the area into such a national punch line that companies no longer wanted to rent office space there.

"I don't think our women like that, not to mention the men," the attaché complained. "We have women ministers, women judges, businesspeople." He pointed out that Kazakh women got the right to vote in 1920, the same year as American women.

The National Conference on Soviet Jewry also came to Kazakhstan's defense, saying the country embraces its "thriving Jewish community" and in 2004 dedicated Central Asia's largest synagogue.

"The president of the country came down, as well as the chief rabbi of Israel," Vassilenko said. "There were all kinds of rabbis from around the world."

But at times the interview by Daniel Radosh veered into the surreal. In disputing Borat's notion that men can buy their brides by exchanging them for insecticide, Vassilenko mentioned an old tradition of kidnapping brides.

"But," Radosh wrote, "he claims that the practice is virtually obsolete. Also, he said, 'If you want to do it for fun, you can do that,' but the woman has to be in on it."

Radosh also quizzed Vassilenko about a Kazakh sport mentioned in travel guides: *kokpar,* a kind of primitive polo:

> When Vassilenko was asked about it, he hesitated, then explained, "That's the one where a goat, a dead goat"—a headless dead goat—"is, um, being held as a sort of a prize. And then one rider has it, and he has to run away with it

from others who seek to catch it and snatch it from him."

"And then," Radosh summed up, "you have a party."

The response to the flap from Sacha's camp was minimal. *The Mirror* quoted a show insider shrugging it off. "Sacha was sending up Americans watching Borat for their lack of knowledge of foreign affairs. It was not a dig at the Kazakhs."

But there did seem to be an effort on the part of others to present Sacha in a positive light. Jason Alper told *People* how Sacha used a picture of his grandmother as his computer's screensaver. "When we're filming and a kid comes over, he gives him mementos from the wardrobe department, like a piece of clothing or a chain. He does a lot for charities."

HBO programming executive Nancy Geller's take was more direct. "He's smart, good-looking, and has a great tush."

Back home in London, the daily tabloids ran breathless articles about the status of Sacha's romance with Isla. In March 2004, the *Daily Mail* reported the couple would be tying the knot "in a Jewish ceremony in Britain . . . after Sacha's devout Jewish parents gave them their blessing."

Fisher, who was to begin filming *Wedding Crashers* the following week in L.A., was quoted in the *Evening Standard* confirming (in tabloidese) that she would "definitely have a Jewish wedding just to be with Sacha. . . . I would do anything—move into any religion—to be united in marriage with him. We have a future together, and religion comes second to love as far as we are concerned."

According to the *Daily Mail,* "There had been reports the couple had problems in their relationship over setting a date. Baron Cohen, 33, is said to have proposed months ago, but had problems finding the time. This was said to be particularly galling for Fisher, 28, who has spent many hours studying Hebrew texts after pledging to convert to Judaism. But when asked when the marriage will happen, she blushed and said: 'I cannot say much more—sorry.'"

However, when Baron Cohen appeared on Howard Stern's show five months later, he made it clear he and Fisher were *not,* in fact, yet engaged. He said they were still merely "dating." He also complained about all the inaccuracies about him and them in the British press. By being so obsessively private, he had invited the alternate curse of misinformation.

Back at the tabs, *Daily Mail* correspondent Nicole Lampert wrote an article describing Sacha and Isla's high life in Hollywood:

> The trappings of transatlantic success include a [\$3.5 million] Beverly Hills home complete with swimming pool which he and actress fi-

ancée Isla Fisher moved into when Jennifer Aniston and her husband Brad Pitt moved out.

Last week, they enjoyed a basketball game, sitting in [$2,000] ringside seats, with Courteney Cox and her husband, David Arquette. Earlier this week, they had a "his and hers" pedicure at a local beauty salon.

While the lifestyle depicted may have had basis in fact, the bigger truth was that Sacha was doing more working than playing. When HBO's *Da Ali G Show* finished its run, both Baron Cohen and Mazer were clearly ready to pursue new challenges. Even before the first episode had aired in 2003, Mazer had predicted, "This new show may well be the last. . . . We honestly don't know." What he did know was that Borat was now the more creatively viable character; Ali G was clearly in his twilight.

Even though he and Sacha were taking a break from their characters, he reassured fans that "Borat will be back and he will loom large once more."

What Mazer didn't reveal was that plans were already under way to take Borat to the big screen. But lessons had been learned from their first foray into taking one of Sacha's characters and adapting them to film. Although *Indahouse* had done well in Britain, where Baron Cohen had a long-established fan base, it generated little interest elsewhere and in the United States had gone straight to video. Part of the reason for the tepid response is that in the movie Ali G had been a tame doppelganger of his television self. The very elements that had made Ali G such a phenomenon—his spontaneity, playing off the guests, his energy, the sense of danger that things might get out of hand at any moment—had been muted by placing the character within the context of strictly defined scenes. In others words, making Sacha stick to a script had cut off Ali G's comedic balls. Mazer and Baron Cohen saw the errors of their creative ways and would not make the same mistake with Borat. They also aimed higher: Instead of a quirky, small-budget independent British film, they wanted a quirky, big-budget Hollywood studio film.

In the spring of 2003, Sacha approached Jay Roach, whose résumé was a comedic Who's Who.* He had directed Mike Myers in the three Austin Powers movies, was director-producer on Ben Stiller's *Meet the Family* and *Meet the Fockers,* and executive-produced *50 First Dates* with Adam Sandler and Drew Barrymore. Roach and Cohen had initially been introduced by their mutual manager, Jimmy Miller.

Roach agreed to coproduce the film. He and Baron Cohen then began to shop the idea around to the studios. They landed at 20th Century Fox, which immediately greenlit the project. The next step was to come up with a director. Sacha met with *South Park* creators Trey Parker and Matt Stone. *South Park*'s subversive, fearless humor felt

*Roach is married to former Bangles lead singer Susanna Hoffs.

like a good fit for Baron Cohen, a longtime admirer of the show.

But Parker and Stone were already committed to making their next feature, *Team America*. So the directing duties eventually went to Todd Phillips, best known for the testosterone-fueled comedies *Old School* and *Road Trip*. Although Phillips's brand of in-your-face comedy seemed out of synch with Sacha's penchant for social satire, the project forged ahead and they began to work on a general story line for the film.

Once they had a loose script in place, they quietly began principal photography. Normally such things are listed in any number of production guides provided by the various entertainment trade publications, such as *Variety* and *Hollywood Reporter*. But this production had intentionally been kept out of the trades and under close wraps, out of fear that too much advance publicity would destroy Sacha's ability to pull the ruse off.

According to *Entertainment Weekly,* "The film's initial concept had shades of *This Is Spinal Tap,* with an American film crew making a documentary about Borat as he traveled across America." But several weeks into the shoot, problems arose. Phillips ultimately dropped out.

The tension between the director's and star's creative visions came to a head at a rodeo in Salem, Virginia. The film crew was there shooting a scene where Borat is supposed to sing the National Anthem prior to the start of the competition. Standing in the middle of the ring,

Borat praised President Bush's war on terror, which was initially cheered. But when Borat said, "I hope you kill every man, woman, and child in Iraq . . . and may George W. Bush drink their blood," the mood of the crowd began to visibly shift.

It turned decidedly ugly when Borat changed the last line of "The Star-Spangled Banner," "and the home of the brave," to "and your home is the grave." According to London's *Daily Mail,* "angry locals in the audience began booing, then fired shots in the air. Rodeo organizers hurriedly escorted Baron Cohen away."

The paper quoted one witness to the event, Robynn Jaymes, commenting, "If he'd been there one minute longer, I think someone would have shot him."

Shortly after the incident, Phillips had abruptly quit the project. There were some reports that Phillips left because of alleged death threats. Others suggested he was worried Sacha's humor was too edgy for him or that Phillips was afraid of being associated with a movie that might be perceived as unpatriotic or anti-American in a post-9/11 envi-

Borat's rendition of "The Star-Spangled Banner" nearly caused a riot.

ronment. Neither Baron Cohen's camp, the studio, nor Phillips would comment at the time.

Even now, the director remains circumspect, saying it was "kind of a long story, but really, truly, the reason why I left is 'cause . . . nobody understands when you say, 'Well, it's creative differences,' that it really is. It boils down to what it was. And they kinda always want something more. I was joking to a friend of mine, I have to figure out something more to say, but really, it was just a direction thing. It was timing, as well as creative differences."

Fox Filmed Entertainment cochairman Jim Gianopulos later went on record, saying, "Ultimately, the creative core of Borat is Sacha. If there were reasons certain elements didn't work out, that was really Sacha's choice."

Reading between those carefully crafted lines, one might infer that the bottom-line answer is Phillips simply didn't have the balls for how far Baron Cohen wanted to push the comedic envelope. Whatever the actual reasons for Phillips's departure, it brought production to an abrupt stop and, possibly worse for Sacha, brought attention to the fact a movie was being filmed at all—even though the studio refused to acknowledge it . . . possibly because they were about to pull the plug.

It doesn't take much to get studio executives nervous, and having a well-known director bail on a project had the brass at 20th Century Fox reassessing the project.

"We were officially a problem project at that point," admits Roach.

A groomed and
coifed Larry Charles

What they needed was a heavy hitter who would both mesh with Baron Cohen and calm the studio's fears. They found their answer in *Seinfeld* and *Curb Your Enthusiasm* veteran Larry Charles, whom Sacha had met at a boxing match. Charles agreed. Sacha was happy . . . but had one favor to ask his new director.

"I had hair down to my ass, a beard down to my waist, and I was wearing pajamas a lot," Charles recalls—a look that in the conservative South just might draw a little unwanted attention. "So Sacha gingerly said to me, 'Would you be willing to possibly, maybe, trim your hair?' I said, 'Of course!' I had to look exactly right so he could do his job."

Finally back on track, Sacha, Charles, Mazer, and a handful of production crew members hit the road in the summer of 2005. Thus began an odyssey that would ultimately take Sacha Baron Cohen to Hollywood's cinematic Promised Land.

# 12

# Filming *Borat*

**I LIKING** U, S, **AND** A a-**very much.** I learn **MANY THINGS**...I was **surprised TO** learn it is **now illegal** to shoot at **RED** Indians...**I would** LIKE to **APOLOGIZE** with **ALL** my heart to **Chief RUNNING Deer AT** the **POTAWATOMI** Casino **IN Nevada.** —Borat

**THERE** had never been a Hollywood studio film quite like *Borat*. With a reported budget of $18 million, there would be none of the requisite creature comforts and conspicuous consumption usually associated with traditional, non-independent productions—no craft services table full of food and drink; no plush trailers; no Town Cars ferrying talent to the location. *Borat* didn't have so much as a Porta Potti. This was unprecedented guerrilla moviemaking for a major studio.

Making *Borat* would also prove to be an exercise in endurance for Sacha. Besides having to live for six weeks with a bristle brush–sized mustache sprouting from his upper lip, for the entire shoot he had to remain in perfect character from the moment he was picked up by the crew van until he got back into his hotel room at night, on average a period of about ten hours. Before going to bed, they would have a writing session to go over the following day's material. It was an exhausting schedule.

"It was hard. . . . I mean, it was a hard film to make," says Baron Cohen. But he believes the effort was necessary "because if somebody gets suspicious and goes, 'Hey, wait a minute . . . he's standing there in the corner like a guy from England' or 'he suddenly sounds like he's not Kazakhi,' then everything is over." Plus, he adds, "I stayed in character because you never know when it is something that's going to be useful. And that happened on a number of occasions."

That led to some interesting encounters with Baron Cohen's own production team. "He and I had some heated discussions, the way a director and actor might, but he'd be chastising me as Borat," Charles remembers. "I'd be standing in the middle of a cotton field in Louisiana being yelled at by Borat."

Contrary to popular opinion, the movie was not just seat-of-the-pants improvisation. There really was a script that was admittedly simple and by necessity loosely constructed: Borat is sent to the United States of America by the Kazakh Ministry of Information to gain a better understanding of American culture. Shortly after arriving in the country, he sees an episode of *Baywatch* and becomes smitten with Pamela Anderson. The rest of the movie is his quixotic quest to find Anderson and make her his wife, believing that will be the only true way to discover the essence of America.

Joining Borat in the cross-country journey is Azamat

Until *Borat,* Davitian was mostly cast in small, unnamed roles: Bartender, Topless Bar Owner, Fat Man, Cabbie, Cab Driver, Taxi Driver, Thug #1, Older Armenian. . . .

Bagatov, his producer-handler-companion. The part was played with such perfect pitch by Ken Davitian that many casting agents and producers assumed he had been imported from Eastern Europe.

Davitian recalls meeting with Disney executives in early 2007. "They said, 'We had no idea you were an American actor.' And I said, 'But I was in *Holes*—one of *your* movies!' "

The irony is that Davitian was raised a few miles from Disney Studios in East Los Angeles and grew up with dreams of being an actor. Born in 1953, he studied theater arts in college and got his first credited part, as the Fat Bartender, in 1977's *American Raspberry*. But rather than pursue an acting career, he went to work at his family's waste-management business.

"With the rubbish money that was coming in we were doing very well," Davitian says. It would be fourteen years before he would go back to acting, driven in part by need after a waste-management venture in Mexico soured and left Davitian bankrupt.

His father-in-law helped Davitian to open the Gotham

Grounds café in Burbank prior to opening The Dip, a mom-and-pop sandwich shop in the Sherman Oaks neighborhood of the San Fernando Valley. With his wife and sons' blessing, Davitian started taking acting classes in the 1990s, found an agent, and started going out on auditions. Since then Davitian has appeared in over forty films and episodes but remained an anonymous journeyman actor. It was his son Robert, then a cinema major at California State University Northridge (CSUN), who first heard Larry Charles was auditioning actors for the role of a "frumpy Eastern European."

"My perfect character!" jokes Davitian. "All my relatives are frumpy Eastern Europeans, Armenians with accents. This is the character I have been doing since I was a child."

Davitian auditioned for Larry Charles and Dan Mazer wearing the same off-the-rack suit he wore in the film, his head shot folded up in his pocket. "I did the audition in character without giving them a résumé or telling them I am an American actor."

It was only when he was ready to leave that he dropped his act—and his accent. He thanked them and said, "If you liked the audition, please call me; I had a great time."

They stopped Davitian before he got to the door.

Because the element of surprise was so integral to the film, the prep work done by the production team before Sacha could get in front of the camera was meticulous. After requesting the interview, the researchers tried to

surreptitiously ferret out whether or not the potential subjects had ever heard of Sacha.

Once they showed up on location to film, the researchers
secured signed release forms from the active participants.
They also gave releases to passersby if the scene was filmed
in a public place.

"We'd have someone in the lobby of a hotel with release
forms," Larry Charles recalls. "We'd tell people we were
shooting today and they may be in the background of a shot."

While the producers don't deny the releases were carefully worded, they maintain the releases are legally bind-
ing. "I don't want to get into the whole process," says Fox
Filmed Entertainment cochairman Jim Gianopulos, "but
people knew in advance they were being taped, so they
signed the appropriate documents."

Director Charles says, "I'd tell people, 'Right now this
movie is only scheduled to be shown in Kazakhstan. I don't
know what they're going to do with it. I'm just here to
shoot it.' We were like the Merry Pranksters in a way.
These people got dosed."

The final step was to have the scene vetted to make sure
they weren't crossing any legal lines. The production had a
lawyer on retainer who advised Charles and Baron Cohen
on how far they could go before breaking a law.

"We're always aware that there's no point in going
through all this, and being heroes, and being as bad as we like
if, ultimately, we can't use what we're shooting," observes
cowriter Peter Baynham.

Despite all the planning, several prospective subjects saw through the ruse. Thanks to the departure of
Todd Phillips, word had trickled out that a movie was
being filmed. Plus, the popularity of the American edi-
tion of *Da Ali G Show* had made Borat a recognizable face
to anyone with HBO—such as the communications director for Georgia Representative Jack Kingston, who
knew what was up the second he heard the interviewer
was from Kazakhstan. Dallas-based *D Magazine*'s Web
site announced that Borat was seen at the Premiere Club
taking boxing lessons. And North Texas radio station
KTCK-AM warned local residents to beware of a hitch-
hiker on Highway 380 after two listeners identified him
as the star of *Da Ali G Show*.

Sometimes Sacha was simply the victim of observant
people. When he was trying to film a scene on a Brooklyn
train using a hidden camera, one of the passengers asked,
"Dude, why does your briefcase have a camera lens?"

But the production had much more success in the Deep
South, partly because the area has less cable penetration than
the rest of the country, so there were fewer people who had
seen the HBO show or who kept up with the entertainment
world quite the way people in large urban areas tended to.

The South is also a more hospitable culture. Sacha said
they found it "ideally suited for Borat because people were
so polite and so welcoming of strangers and also so proud
of their American heritage that they would talk to this

person about American society and about American values for an hour and a half."

And even there some questioned the veracity of the interview. "Sometimes people would say, 'Is this real?'" Charles says. "I'd say, 'Yes, it's totally real.' And in my mind I'm thinking, *It may not be the reality you think it is, but trust me, it's real. There's film in the camera.*"

That said, Charles insists:

> I never felt like we tricked anyone in a cruel way. We gave people a chance to be themselves. . . . When we were making the film, we had this almost Talmudic questioning of ourselves. "Who are we? What do we really believe? How far are we willing to go? What is our line in the sand that we're not willing to cross?" We were constantly asking ourselves, "Are we being fair? Do the ends justify the means?"

They tried to stay clear of using anyone who would appear helpless or weak on film. "We tried to explore the aristocracy, the elite, the vain, the egomaniacal—that was one of our lines in the sand."

To get his subjects to open up, Sacha says, Borat had to ultimately be believable. "The challenge, the interesting thing about the structure of this movie is that in each scene we had two things we had to accomplish: Each scene had to be funny, but it also had to achieve a certain story beat to push the story forward."

The idea of using Anderson as the catalyst for the movie's overall plot "came about very early," Sacha recalls. "She was the epitome of the American dream, really, this blond silicone television star," and gave Borat a purpose and a reason for traveling cross-country. "We chose quite deliberately."

Baron Cohen calls the film experimental in that unscripted reactions were essential to push forward a (loosely) scripted plot. "Even though the end result is experimental, the initial structure is quite traditional. It's a movie with a three-act structure. We're just making it work in the real world. It's a fusion of the two. That was the constant struggle, really . . . to get the funny but also to get the plot point."

Mazer says that after doing this kind of comedy for eight years, they had it refined to a sharp comedic point by the time they filmed the movie. "It's an incredibly difficult and unique skill, the actual writing of it. . . . All our jokes are tightly honed and tightly written, and Sacha delivers them brilliantly and also improvises around the situation."

Borat's reactions were by then second nature to Baron Cohen, notes Mazer, "which means that he can react and he can go with it. And it's beyond an acting job; it's a complete immersion."

"The principle that we use is, we go in as scripted as

possible," adds Baron Cohen. "But then you've also got to be prepared to throw everything away if new opportunities present themselves."

The writers agree that nobody is more willing than Sacha to go with the flow. "It's very rare for Sacha to say no," notes Baynham. "I don't believe we've ever rejected a situation outright, from our side or from Sacha's side— except when they won't insure us to do it."

Sacha recalls a scene where Borat gets lost in Mexico, his van breaks down, and his exhaust pipe breaks off. "Borat starts carrying the exhaust pipe, and it's extremely hot; he's walking through the desert. He takes a towel, wraps it around his head, and it looks like he's a mujahadeen operative with a rocket launcher over his shoulder. And then the idea was for Borat to walk across the border and straight into Minutemen."

The studio would not sign off on the scene because they felt it was too dangerous. But, Sacha says, "we only got word of that *after* we shot the scene."

But the studio's concern was valid, admits Mazer. "There were quite a lot of situations where you just had to think very hard. You want to do it—you always want to do it, whatever the risks are. But then you assess. What backup do we need? What protection do you need? If you want a scene where he goes into a very scary situation and says things to scary people, you just back up and occasionally don't do it."

If the movie is any indication, those occasions are rare.

At the rodeo that proved Todd Phillips's undoing, the Salem, Virginia, Civic Center's assistant director, John Saunders, told the local newspaper that if Sacha and his crew had not gotten away when they did, "there would have been a riot," he was convinced. "They would have been killed."

In the movie, the rodeo's producer, Bobby Rowe, has an exchange with Borat about gays:

Borat:   They hang them in my country.

Rowe:   That's what we're trying to do here.

Rowe later tried to explain himself to *Salon.com*. "As long as [homosexuals] don't mess with me and get me involved, if that's their choice, just have at it. Just don't come in my household and try to demand, as they're doing now, all sorts of things—all this marriage and this mess. If you want to go live together, go live together, but don't drag everyone else into it. It's, like, before you could just pump your gas, but the thieves ruined it for everyone. Now everyone has to go pay for their gas first. Homosexuals, they want their rights for marriage and all this stuff, and they want respectability. If you want to live that life, live that life, but don't involve the whole rest of the country."

Such a response efficiently proves Baron Cohen's point that political correctness hasn't diminished bigotry, it's simply forced it underground where it's more dangerous.

The uncovering of those attitudes is why Larry Charles, who is Jewish, stresses that *Borat* isn't simply a funny movie but is an important look at ourselves as a culture. As an example, he uses the scene where Borat goes into a gun store asking for a recommendation on the best gun to kill Jews: "This gun-store guy doesn't hesitate: 'I'd recommend a 9mm or a Glock automatic.'"

"That's one of those moments when you're going, *Holy shit—that just really happened*. This anti-Semitism is real and it comes from ignorance. You understand it better and maybe in some way that will ultimately defuse it."

The film's producer, Jay Roach, observes, "Political correctness has led to a more civil society because people with racist attitudes have taken them underground. It's a fascinating social experiment to observe this character walking amongst us, revealing this."

Ironically, some felt Borat didn't go far enough. Grace Welch, a yoga instructor who was one of the Veteran Feminists of America, says, "What he does, he does very well, so I don't feel anger. I was inclined very much to laugh at the event." But she felt that the movie "didn't make the point with sexism that perhaps he did with anti-Semitism and homophobia."

Not every scene sought to showcase the worst in people. When Borat is at his lowest point after discovering Pamela Anderson is not a virgin, the script called for him to seek solace at an evangelical revival meeting. "We needed a scene where he'd leave the end of Act II reinvigorated with life and with this renewed sense of purpose—a renewed mission to wed and bed Pamela Anderson," Sacha explains. When writing the scenes, Sacha and his team would determine what they needed from the scene and then try to anticipate what kinds of reactions they would get. In the case of the revival, their anticipation was almost completely on point, with the pastor saying almost exactly what they had predicted—that Jesus was there to save Borat. "That man was such a fundamentalist he became predictable."

Less expected was Baron Cohen's personal reaction while filming the scene. He says: "You have about six men pressing on you at the time. I had a man on either side, holding my arms, and they start shaking your arms so it looks like you're possessed or you're suddenly seized by this greater force. And then there's not much oxygen; the pastor was shouting at me, 'You can speak in tongues now; you can speak in tongues.' So when you actually start moving your tongue and start, they are so excited, it's this really overwhelming experience."

Many of the people Borat encountered showed almost preternatural patience, like the antique store owner Larry Walker, who saw five hundred dollars' worth of his inventory get smashed when Borat fell into display cases.

"I knew where those antiques were and I knew I had one chance to knock over all the cheapest antiques in the shop. We had intentionally positioned all the cheapest antiques in one particular area of the shop so that the scene wouldn't cost too much money and so that we really wouldn't cause too much upset to the people there."

Walker says, "You have to laugh at it now. But at the time, we were just glad to get rid of him."

Probably not nearly as much as the diners at the Magnolia Springs Manor in Helena, Alabama, were. Besides Borat's verbal barrage of malapropisms and glib insults, he pushes the normally genteel group to the breaking point with one of the more jaw-dropping stunts in the film—Borat presenting a bag of his feces at the dinner table.

In a Q&A with *Written By,* Mazer says he and the other writers—Art Hines and Peter Baynham—dissected the scene at length prior to filming it.

> Mazer: That debate over the nature of the bag, we get incredibly—I suppose "anal" is the wrong word to use about the shit.
>
> Baynham: I'd never spoken for an hour about what kind of bag we should use to put our piece of shit in. And I'm sitting there thinking, *This is my job.* . . .
>
> Hines: I'd say the unsung hero in this production is Jason Alper. . . . He has a credit on the movie: FECES PROVIDED BY JASON ALPER.

Mazer said the time was well spent "because it's a brilliant moment. It would have been probably too disgusting if it was a completely clear bag. And it would have been not that funny if it was entirely opaque."

For her birthday, Sacha gave Luenell a day at the Burke Williams spa in L.A.

Sacha admits the scene gave him pause. "Everyone is having a lovely time downstairs, but I'm about to bring a bag of fresh feces to the table. There is that moment when you look in the mirror and . . . you almost feel like a hit man."

Most fascinating is that it wasn't the proud display of excrement that most upset his dinner companions—it was the appearance of the black prostitute.

The hooker was played by actress/comedienne Luenell Campbell.* It was one of the few times the writers did not anticipate the response they got, admits Baynham. "The scene was supposed to go on longer and he [Borat] was supposed to take her to the bathroom and have sex with her."

The plan was to shoot the guests' reactions as they listened to the sounds of Borat and the prostitute going at it. When he was finished, Borat would come out and ask to

---

*Professionally she is known simply as Luenell. On her Web site, www .heyluenell.com, you can see a photo of her and an out-of-character Sacha. When MTV asked about her participation in the film, Luenell was coy: "I can't tell you about any of the inner workings. I'm sworn to secrecy. . . ."

borrow thirty dollars to pay her. They assumed at that point he'd be asked to leave, says Hines. "And then he'd have to come back because he'd left his underpants in the bathroom and could he have his underpants back?"

But the scene was over before it had a chance to begin. "When the prostitute came in, they reacted so violently just to a black woman being in the house that that was it," recalls Mazer. "We never envisioned they would react that violently simply to her presence. So they threw them out immediately, and we didn't get a chance to do that funny set piece."

Remarkably, not everyone who attended the dinner held a grudge. Mike Jared told *Salon.com,* "All things considered, we got out of this pretty clean." Presbyterian minister Cary Speaker, whose wife was positively apoplectic in later interviews (see chapter 14), has since shrugged it off. "Hey, he fooled us; it's funny. Watching this, I'm sure it's funny [to some people]," including Speaker's two grown sons. "It was just not funny that night."

A former producer for Jackson, Mississippi's WAPT wasn't laughing, either. Dharma Arthur told *Newsweek* Baron Cohen had basically ruined her life after his appearance on an afternoon news program. "Because of him, my boss lost faith in my abilities and second-guessed everything I did thereafter," she complained. "I spiraled into depression, and before I could recover, I was released from my contract early." Arthur says she was out of work for three months, got deep into debt, and was worried about losing her home. "How upsetting that a man who leaves so much harm in his path is lauded as a comedic genius."

Some might find it equally upsetting that a news producer doesn't bother to thoroughly vet a potential guest's credentials—Arthur admitted she failed to research Mr. Borat before putting him on the air.

But the station's GM, Stuart Kellogg, told the Jackson *Clarion-Ledger,* "We were gotten. Our folks researched the production company, which has its own Web site and sounds legitimate. They did their homework, but not well enough. It seemed plausible that he was who he said he was. Who knows what an accent from Kazakhstan sounds like?" Granted, but the experience still led WAPT to revise its policy on background checks and to fire Arthur.

Easily the most talked-about scene in the film was the nude fight/wrestling scene with Azamat that occurs after Borat catches him beating off while looking at Pamela Anderson in the *Baywatch Annual* magazine.

"It was crucial that the *Baywatch Annual* had almost the significance of the ring in *Lord of the Rings,*" Sacha explains. "That gives the naked wrestling a lot more weight because Azamat is then desecrating this sacred object."

Mazer marvels at how Sacha is "willing to go out and do the most obscene things. It's very rare that you find somebody who will go, 'OK, yeah, all right,' and have a naked fight. To abandon vanity in favor of comedy is a very rare thing for somebody to have."

"He has no inhibitions with his physical self. None whatsoever," agrees producer Roach. "When you think of the green thong to the little gym shorts, there's very little concern for the risk of looking uncool."

According to author Harry Medved, a hotel employee confirmed that the wrestling scene was filmed at the Los Angeles Airport Hilton. Thinking back, Sacha says he's lucky to have made it out alive.

"There was a little sign that I was going to show Larry Charles, which was that when I ran out of air when Ken was sitting on my face, I would tap on the bed three times," he said. And in the film you see Borat repeatedly tapping the bed. "But Larry was so engrossed in looking at the monitor that he didn't notice I was dying under Ken's anus."

Davitian says that Sacha's one request prior to filming the scene was "that I shower . . . and shower . . . and then shower again . . . then powder and shower again."

The five-five, three-hundred-pound actor admits he tried unsuccessfully to wear a pair of boxers for the scene. "I kept saying, 'Fat, naked guy: not funny. That's a Wes Craven movie. Fat guy in boxers: hilarious.'"

In the end, he said, he bared it all because "if the genius is gonna get naked, I am following the genius." Davitian says that working with Sacha was a comfortable fit. "I don't want to sound immodest, but I thought . . . there is a chemistry between this tall, skinny Cambridge-educated genius and the short, fat guy. It works!"*

One unexpected glitch was that the apparent adrenaline rush to survive caused by his near-death experience under Davitian's ample weight gave Sacha a bit of an erection. So in post-production a (rather long) black rectangle was superimposed over Borat's penis in order to prevent an NC-17 rating.

Modesty, clearly, is not much of an issue with Sacha. Another scene in the script called for Borat to visit a plastic surgeon in order to have a foreskin sewn back on so Pamela Anderson won't think he's Jewish. He dropped his pants and presented his penis for inspection . . . only to have the doctor recognize him.

"Wait! You're Ali G! You're Ali G! You used to be on HBO! You're Ali G!"

So that scene was added to the outtakes pile.

While the majority of scenes cut from the final edit were removed because of time considerations or because they didn't meet the "funny" standard, one scene—filmed at a porno shoot—was cut, Mazer says, because it was an "unbelievably shocking, amazing, graphic, extreme scene."

Although he won't get into specifics—and shrugs non-committally when asked point-blank if Sacha actually en-

---

*When the script called for them to be speaking Kazakh to each other, Davitian spoke Armenian while Sacha spoke Hebrew. Davitian says he had no idea what Baron Cohen was saying.

gaged in sexual activity—Mazer says that with the wrestling scene already in the movie, it simply would have been too much.

On the Huffington Post online site, Paul Krassner describes part of the scene: "Borat wouldn't have sex with [a porn actress] because her vagina was shaved. To solve the problem, he cuts locks of his own hair off and pastes them to her crotch. . . . But this scene was eliminated, not only because of ratings-fear, but also because it would have been inconsistent with the scene where he tells a car dealer he wants to buy a car that [has] a *pussy magnet* for a woman who *shave down there*."

It's no wonder Larry Charles says the production team frequently found themselves in one form of jeopardy or another. "We walked into extremely hostile situations that we then exacerbated into *incredibly* hostile situations," he recalls affably.

Sacha acknowledges that their run-ins with the police were making the shoots especially difficult. "The first time I got stopped by the police, I thought to myself, *What do I do?* because I was separated from the crew. And I thought, *There can't be a law against speaking in a funny voice to a policeman.* Plus, I didn't know what story the rest of the crew had told the police since they'd separated all of us."

Charles recalls the time they were passing in front of the White House and got pulled over by the Secret Service. "And Sacha stayed in character: He asked them what organization they were from, and they said, 'Secret Service,' and he said, 'Like KGB?' "

Baron Cohen dryly notes, "We were driving in an ice-cream van past the White House, so we were clearly Al-Qaeda." By his own count, Sacha says they had over forty encounters with law enforcement. "And that ranged from the NYPD to the FBI to the Secret Service. And whenever they stopped me, I stayed in character, because I never knew if it was something we could use for the actual movie."

So the number-one priority for the crew was to prevent, at any cost, Sacha from getting arrested. If he was arrested and deported, the movie was history. While filming in Manhattan, they shot a scene where Borat assumes he gets to keep the room's furniture because the bill is so high. When the hotel manager saw Borat walking through the lobby clutching his comforter and the alarm clock, he promptly called the police. The line producer and first AD ended up spending the night in jail. But by the time a warrant was issued for Sacha's arrest, he was safely out of state, holed up in a New Jersey hotel.

In Louisiana a woman whose family had once owned a plantation was so offended by Borat she called the police. "I think I might have been trying to sell her some Kazakhi slaves," Sacha says. "We had thirty seconds to make our getaway in an ice-cream truck whose top speed was fifty miles per hour."

His worst moment did not make it into the film.

Out of money, Borat takes a job as a door-to-door sales-
man. He asks one family member if he could please use
the bathroom. After several minutes, he comes out naked,
"except wrapped in their towel. He's holding one of their
toothbrushes, going, 'Now, uh, which toothpaste can I
use?' at which point I was thrown out of the house by this
family." Sacha was still standing in front of the house
when he heard police sirens. "And I'm looking to the director going: 'Vat do I do?' My costume is in
the bathroom of this house, I'm standing in a towel
that doesn't belong to me." He considered taking off
in their production van but realized that leaving in their
towel "means I am stealing some property so I can be done
for theft. However, if I take the towel off, I can be done
for indecent exposure, so I was in this terrible dilemma."

He jumped into the van and called their attorney. "Finally
I was taken to this safe location and we negotiated to get the
costume back—and the underpants."

While there has been much speculation on whether or
not Pamela Anderson was in on the joke, she most certainly was an active participant. But the notion she was a
hapless victim decidedly feeds into the outrageousness of
*Borat*. When asked by MTV News, Anderson was evasive:
"I can't really say. I'm sworn to secrecy," adding, "I love
Sacha; he's such a nice guy. He's the new Monty Python."*

---

*Note to Anderson: Monty Python was not actually an individual. . . .

Larry Charles was equally vague. "All I can say was that she was extremely good-humored about what happened to her."

Dismissed at the time as another example of tabloid hyperbole, in August 2005 rumors surfaced about Pamela Anderson conducting a "commitment ceremony" for her two dogs: Star, a golden retriever, and Luca, a chihuahua. It was subsequently reported at TV.com that

> Cohen, in character as Kazakhstani TV reporter Borat, wore shorts with a leather jacket and cap and brandished a white *keytar*. Once ashore, the oft-reviled comedian sprinted toward Anderson and felled her with a perfectly executed rugby tackle, causing her to drop the beloved Luca. . . . Bodyguards seized the interloper, dragged him back to the shore, and dunked him in the hungry waves. The wedding party quickly composed itself, and the ceremony continued without further incident.

From the mere fact they had shot another scene together, one can comfortably infer that Anderson was in cahoots with the production. That scene, and many others, never made it into the final eighty-three-minute film. Larry Charles says he shot over four hundred hours of footage. The first rough cut of *Borat* came in at an eye-crossing six hours, prompting Charles to comment: "There'll be a lot of bonus footage when the DVD comes out."

The decision of what stayed in and what didn't was based on several factors, such as whether it was too similar to another bit already in, whether it moved the story along, and if it was deemed funny enough. But the connective tissue, as far as Charles is concerned, was Sacha. He compared Baron Cohen's performance in *Borat* to Marlon Brando's in *On the Waterfront* because of its groundbreaking nature. "Before that, everything was stylized, the John Barrymore school. After that, you couldn't act in the old style anymore. I believe that Sacha's performance does the same thing.

"He is an incredibly intense, focused individual."

Whether or not Baron Cohen will fundamentally change comic acting remains to be seen. But it is inarguable that the movie was poised, some say purposely, to generate a firestorm of controversy, with Sacha squarely in the middle of it.

# 13

# Sacha Emerges

**MY** parents **ARE** incredibly **loving.** And **I** think **THAT** gives **YOU** the **strength** to go **out** into a **CROWD** of **people** who **hate you** . . . probably, **IF YOU** want **TO analyze** it. **—SACHA** Baron **COHEN**

**WHILE** Charles and Mazer immersed themselves for the next year in the daunting task of post-production, Baron Cohen found himself doing double duty as *Borat* producer and working actor. In May 2005, the animated *Madagascar* was released, in which Sacha provided the voice of Julien, the lemur king. He also appeared in the fifth-season finale of *Curb Your Enthusiasm,* where he and Dustin Hoffman play Larry David's not-so-angelic guides to Heaven.

The biggest boost to Baron Cohen's U.S. film career was being cast in *Talladega Nights: The Ballad of Ricky Bobby* as Bobby's bitter racing rival, Jean Girard. Filmed on location in North Carolina and at Talladega Superspeedway in Talladega, Alabama, the movie took Baron Cohen back to some of his *Borat* haunts, with amusingly similar results.

When Will Ferrell's character was introduced at Talladega, the crowd roared its approval. When Sacha, who played an arrogant French racer, was announced, the two hundred thousand spectators in the stands loudly booed. Sacha wasn't fazed. "So it was the second time in Alabama I was booed out by a crowd of over sixty thousand people," he muses.

To prepare for the role, Baron Cohen and Ferrell spent a day at the NASCAR training school at Lowe's Motor Speedway in Charlotte, North Carolina—the same track where Britney Spears had previously spent a day and posted a speed of 112 miles per hour. Their only goal was to beat her time.

But, Ferrell admits, when he and Sacha showed up, "we were so frightened watching the cars go around and so vocal about it that the instructor told us to be quiet 'cause we were scaring the people that actually paid the money to do the school.

"It was terrifying, but once you go around a couple of times you get used to the speed. And we beat Britney's time."

*Talladega Nights* went on to earn $150 million in the United States—the eleventh-highest-grossing film of 2006—and critics singled out Baron Cohen's performance. *Rolling Stone* called his camp, Camus-reading Jean Girard "delicious . . . inspired lunacy."

Critics were less kind about Baron Cohen's appearance at the 2006 MTV Awards. In character as Borat, he greeted the audience with a cheery: "Good evening, gentlemen and prostitutes." Then while introducing a performance by Gnarls Barkley, he sent a shout-out to

Jessica Simpson: "Jessica, you have a beautiful mouth. I could see it very clearly through your denim shorts . . . I like!"

Sacha was also causing a stir out of character. By that time, Sacha and Isla Fisher were finally officially engaged and he seemed more bent than ever on keeping his private life out of the public eye. The *Daily News* reported that Baron Cohen assaulted photographer Richard Corkery with a "one-handed martial arts–style hold" the night of the *Wedding Crashers* premiere when he tried to take a picture of Sacha and Isla. Corkery said that Baron Cohen warned him to ask permission first before taking any photos.

"It was scary to me," *New York Times* reporter Paula Schwartz said. "All of a sudden, Ali came racing up, and his hand went up on Dick's throat, neck, his windpipe."

Sacha's publicist, Matt Labov, denied that characterization of the encounter, claiming Baron Cohen "did not put a hand on Dick. He put his hand in front of the camera but did not touch him."

In the weeks leading up to *Borat*'s release, Baron Cohen made dozens of personal appearances, all in character. Mazer had kept Baynham and Hines on board to write original material for Baron Cohen's talk show guest spots and personal appearances.

"You go on these high-profile talk shows, you do Leno, then you can't do that material on Letterman. You go on

*The Daily Show* and you can't do that material on *Conan,*" Mazer explains. They also did movie junkets in New York and Britain. "It's just this tidal wave of material you've got to generate, isn't it? And people have literally said, 'What does Borat think of Philadelphia?' And you've got to have answers."

Baynham recalls the time Borat visited *Live with Regis and Kelly*. "It was sheer madness. We were out with Regis Philbin, walking around the streets of New York, he takes Borat to this hot-dog stand, and there were people shouting from buses, 'Hey, Borat! Hey, Regis!' in equal measures. We were walking backward in front of them, writing the shit down on boards and holding up stuff for him to say."

For all the effort Sacha put into promoting *Borat,* the best publicity came courtesy of the Kazakh government. The movie's release rekindled the country's long-running denouncement of Baron Cohen's characterization, which had crescendoed in November 2005, when Borat's appearance at the MTV Awards so outraged the Kazakh Foreign Ministry that spokesman Yerzhan Ashykbayev threatened legal action. The government called Borat's character "a concoction of bad taste and ill manners . . . completely incompatible with the ethics and civilized behavior of Kazakhstan's people."

Sacha was in Los Angeles working on the film's post-production when he heard the news. Borat wasted no time responding:

In response to Mr. Ashykbayev's comments, I'd like to state I have no connection with Mr. Cohen and fully support my government's decision to sue this Jew. . . . Kazakhstan is as civilized as any other country in the world. Women can now travel on inside of bus, homosexuals no longer have to wear blue hats, and age of consent has been raised to 8 years old. . . . We have incredible natural resources, hardworking labor, and some of the cleanest prostitutes in whole of Central Asia.

Public war of words aside, Baron Cohen admitted he was surprised at the ill feelings. "The joke is on people who can believe that the Kazakhstan that I describe can exist."

The rhetoric continued into November 2006. Erlan Idrissov, U.K. ambassador for Kazakhstan, complained that "Sacha Baron Cohen has developed a grotesque character who mocks many people in this society and my own. What I saw of the film was not Kazakhstan. He used village people from a very remote part of Eastern Europe. I am also very sorry for the people who acted in Borat's film because he used them for his own self-promotion.

"And also I felt sorry for the Americans he duped in his film, that was an utterly rude mocking of American society. I couldn't get rid of a small feeling of being insulted by the film."

The country also pulled the plug on Borat's Kazakh Web site, www.borat.kz.

"We've done this so he can't badmouth Kazakhstan under the .kz domain name," Nurlan Isin, president of the Association of Kazakh IT Companies, told Reuters at the time. "He can go and do whatever he wants at other domains."

Going on a PR offensive, the Kazakh government took out a very expensive four-page ad in *The New York Times* promoting their native soil with factoids such as: "The country is home to the world's largest population of wolves." (The ad may have cost as much as $400,000.)

Of course, all it did was give Baron Cohen more comic fodder. When Kazakh president Nursultan Nazarbayev arrived in Washington for a diplomatic visit, Borat and his camera crew stationed themselves outside the White House. There he invited "Supreme Warlord Premier George Walter Bush . . . O. J. Simpson . . . and Melvin Gibsons" to a screening of the movie.

"At first, Kazakh censors wouldn't let me release this movie because of anti-Semitism, but then they decided that there was just enough."

Later, Baron Cohen reflected on the surrealism of being declared a sovereign nation's most dangerous enemy. "It's inherently a comic situation. I mean, it's always risky when you don't go down the normal route. I wish I would've been there at the briefing that Bush got about who I am, who Borat is. It would have had to be great."

But not everyone agreed with the official state party line. Politician Dariga Nazarbayeva, who is also the Kazakh president's daughter, went on national television and defended Sacha, pointing out that his Web site "damaged our image much less than its closure, which was covered by all global news agencies." She also told her countrymen, "We should not be afraid of humor and we shouldn't try to control everything."

Brandchannel.com writer Abram Sauer noted, "Kazakhstan should see this as an opportunity to, in a manner of speaking, put itself on the map in the minds of wealthy Western tourists. It is hard to argue that Borat may be harming the image of a country that had no image to begin with."

When Kazakh officials finally realized they were becoming the butt of their own ill humor they pulled an abrupt about-face. Reuters quoted deputy foreign minister Rakhat Aliyev as saying, "I understand that the feelings of many people are hurt by Cohen's show but we must have a sense of humor and respect the creative freedom of others."

Novelist Sapabek Asip-uly urged the Kazakhstan Club of Art Patrons to honor Baron Cohen with its annual award. In a letter to the *Vremya* newspaper Asip-uly said Borat "has managed to spark an immense interest of the whole world in Kazakhstan—something our authorities could not do during the years of independence. If state officials completely lack a sense of humor, their country becomes a laughing stock." The reconciliation seemed complete when President Nazarbayev agreed that the movie had raised Kazakhstan's global profile.

Larry Charles, for one, would love to accept the government's invitation to visit. "Even if we got shot down on the tarmac . . . that's pretty good bonus material for the DVD."

*Borat* opened November 3, 2006, as the surprise number-one movie, earning over $26 million in a paltry 831 theaters, for a gaudy per screen average in excess of $31,000—the third highest per-theater average of all time for movies opening on five hundred screens or more, behind *Pirates of the Caribbean: Dead Man's Chest* and *Spider-Man*. The film that had been expected to dominate that weekend, Disney's *The Santa Clause 3: The Escape Clause,* was a distant second.

But the film's success inflamed the debate over Borat's anti-Semitism and Baron Cohen's personal responsibility as a Jew. The Anti-Defamation League issued a statement saying that while it understood Sacha's intentions, it feared that "the audience may not always be sophisticated enough to get the joke."

Jay Roach did not share the ADL's concerns. "If you want the anti-Semitism to be clearly anti-anti-Semitism, you have to exaggerate it. You have to take it so far that there's no ambiguity about how ridiculous it is."

But Richard B. Jewell, a USC professor of film history, agreed with the ADL. "I can almost guarantee you that not everyone will get the joke," he told *The New York Times,* adding, "In my opinion it's a very healthy thing. Some of best films that have been made in the last fifty years have been black comedies."

He used *Dr. Strangelove* as an example. "What can be more serious? It makes people think about these things in ways they don't when there are more straightforward, serious, sober films."

Many film historians agreed that Hollywood didn't have the best track record when it came to addressing anti-Semitism head-on.

"Hollywood has a history of avoiding controversial topics, and notably did so at the end of the 1930s, with the rise of Nazism and anti-Semitism," says UCLA associate film professor Jonathan Kuntz. Studios, he explains, "were afraid of offending audiences, and of limiting their popularity in the European market. And because so many moguls were Jewish, they were afraid this would be used to attack Hollywood as anti-Nazi."

*New York Times* writer Sharon Waxman pointed out that today Hollywood is still "often reluctant to openly discuss anti-Semitism, as was evidenced by the careful debate over Mel Gibson's 2004 blockbuster, *The Passion of the Christ.* Only when Mr. Gibson was heard making anti-Jewish slurs this summer during a drunken-driving arrest did a few Hollywood veterans speak out against him."

The criticism that Baron Cohen was irresponsible and insensitive brought peers to his defense, to applaud Sacha's refusal to compromise his artistic and comedic vision:

> Ricky Gervais (*The Office* star and creator):
> "Borat is fantastic. He absolutely goes all
> out. If he can justify something, he doesn't
> compromise." As for Sasha, whom he has
> known since *The 11 O'Clock Show,* "he's not like
> what you'd expect. He's very scholarly and
> quiet, and serious."

> Stephen Colbert (host of *The Colbert Report*):
> "He's courageous. It's hard to know how
> much someone knows what he's doing is real
> and how much is a creation. I have a great
> admiration for him. It takes a tremendous
> amount of guts to stick to your character."

> Paul Rudd (*Friends*): "He's got more guts and
> is more inventive than anyone except Peter
> Sellers. I actually, as a diehard Peter Sellers
> fan, think he might actually be better, because
> he's a very nice guy, too."

Stand-up comic Kathy Griffin thinks it's funny that "people are saying he shines a negative light on American culture because you know what? Sometimes America has a negative light. That's why it's funny. A positive light is not funny.

"When I started out I thought, *Oh, I can never talk about AIDS, I can never talk about cancer,*" she recalls. "And then I met AIDS patients and cancer patients, and they told me the sickest jokes. It was the first thing out of their mouths. And I thought, *What am I worried about?* And frankly, if you're worrying about people's feelings you kind of can't do the job."

Bill Maher, who had his show *Politically Incorrect* canceled by ABC after he proved to be too politically incorrect for late-night broadcast television, says, "My bristles go up when I hear somebody complain about crossing the line. Let the audience decide. An audience is very quick to tell a comedian when they feel he has crossed the line. They don't laugh, or they boo.

"One of my favorite types of laughs," Maher says, "is the kind where you can almost feel this harpoon go through [the audience], because it was so true, but then they laughed. They didn't want to laugh. It's that to-the-bone. The great thing about laughter is that it's an involuntary response."

Writer Paul Mooney, who has worked with Richard Prior and Dave Chappelle, stresses that "comedy is the funniest when it's mean and shocking. If you study African-American comedy, it's always been politically incorrect because it's always been politically incorrect to be a Negro. Moms Mabley, Redd Foxx . . . they were as mean and nasty as you could find—and they were great."

The *Aristocrats*[*] director Paul Provenza points out that "it's very important to understand that Sacha Baron Cohen doesn't feel the way that Borat feels, and that's why it's comedy."

And by all accounts, Baron Cohen the man is indeed the anti-Borat. "He's one of the least neurotic, most engaging people that I've encountered in the performing arts," says Roach. "I find him to be incredibly intelligent, articulate, charming, super-polite by American standards. You almost need to see him as the English-accented, baritone-voiced guy he really is so you can recognize what a transformation every one of those characters is."

But good intentions notwithstanding, secondhand platitudes can sound like lifeless press releases. Clearly, it was time for Sacha to come out from behind his safety net—"I've got to take off the mustache and reveal the real me"—and in late 2006 he began giving selected interviews.

It was equally clear the process was painful, as he admitted to *Rolling Stone* writer Neil Strauss when apologizing for worrying about comments he made about Kazakhstan:

---

[*]Frequently called the filthiest joke ever, "The Aristocrats" has been told by comics since vaudeville. The joke has three main parts: The setup is a family act going to see an agent. The "act" is then described, the goal being to come up with the most offensive, obscene scenario imaginable (bestiality, incest, and amputees are some of the more popular themes). When the stunned agent says, "That's quite an act . . . what do you call yourselves?" the punch line is always: "The Aristocrats!" Check out Penn (of Penn & Teller) Jillette's blog at www.thearistocrats.com.

Sorry I've been so overcautious, but these things start to gather a lot of weight and importance when you put them off for years and years. . . . Literally, it was terrifying agreeing to do this.

Baron Cohen considers himself a private person and has found fame a difficult intrusion to handle. "So I've been trying to have my cake and eat it, too; to have my character be famous yet still lead a normal life where I'm not trapped by fame and recognizability," he explains. "I guess I've been greedy. Maybe it's time to let go."

Staying in character allowed Sacha to do the outrageous things his comedy required, things that Sacha Baron Cohen would find difficult—if not impossible—to do. However, there is an advantage in dropping the Borat guise. "It's exhausting [staying in character] because there's a greater pressure to be funny if you turn up somewhere as your comic character."

While Sacha took the opportunity of the interviews to explain his feeling about Borat's anti-Semitism, he made no apologies: "I think part of the movie shows the absurdity of holding any form of racial prejudice, whether it's hatred of African-Americans or of Jews." He pointed out that *Borat* was one of the most successful comedies of all time in Israel, and that the movie sometimes even got standing ovations when it played. He said he suspected that Israelis might have been reacting positively to the fact that when

Borat "speaks in Kazakh," he is actually speaking in a blend of Hebrew and Polish. And who wouldn't love the delicious irony of the cheerfully anti-Semetic Borat spewing his anti-Semitism in the language of the Jews?

Although Sacha does not characterize himself as particularly religious, Roach said following certain Jewish traditions was important to him. "If it's an emergency, he'll answer an e-mail. But he really does shut down on Friday nights and Saturdays." When Baron Cohen hosted *Saturday Night Live* in 2006, Roach acknowledged that "it wasn't without plenty of discussion."

As 2006 drew to a close, Sacha sounded like a man needing a break. But there was no time for a vacation. The film's unqualified popular success, with over £130 million in worldwide box office, made Baron Cohen a cinematic hot property, and he waded through the offers flooding in—along with the lawsuits. As 2007 dawned, *Borat* was poised to become one of the most litigated movies in Hollywood history.

# 14

# A Litigation
# Firestorm

You **MEAN** the **PERSON** **that** put **PLASTIC** **FIST** in my **anus** is **homosexual?**—BORAT

**IT** got to the point where it seemed hardly a day went by without someone new announcing they were suing Baron Cohen and/or 20th Century Fox. One of the first to threaten litigation was Mahir Cagri, based in Ismir, Turkey. Cagri claimed to be the original Borat. He gained his fifteen minutes of cyber fame in 1999 when his Web site—and catchphrases "I Kiss You!" and "I Like Sex!"— became a kitchy sensation. His penchant for wearing red Speedos and waxing poetic about his love of the accordion was spoofed by the likes of David Letterman and *MadTV*. CNET ranked his site number two on their Top Ten Web Fads list, while in 2006 *PC Magazine* included Mahir's salute to Mahir as one of the 25 worst Web sites ever.

In November 2006, *Wired* magazine ran an interview with Mahir, who announced he was planning to sue Baron Cohen for using him as the basis for the Borat character.

In a later e-mail to Electronic News Network, Cagri groused, "All people know Sacha Baron Cohen imitate

Mahir to Borat: "I Sue You!"
© Mahir Cagri

only me. He is stealing my character and giving bad message to USA people. . . . He never contacted me or got my permission. The bombshell is going to fall. [Baron Cohen] is making money by using me. If possible you can help me too for stop this or find good lawyer?"

The only problem for Cagri is that Borat's first appearance on Channel 4 predated the "I Kiss You!" Web site by several years, making some suspect it was more likely Borat was the inspiration for Cagri's online persona.

While Mahir's claims seemed primarily ego-boosting self-promotion, several of the people burned in *Borat* took their grievances to court. Two of the three Chi Psi frat brothers from the University of South Carolina featured in the film sued the studio. Identified in court papers as Justin Seay and Christopher Rotunda, they claimed the movie's portrayal of them after they picked Borat up hitchhiking "made plaintiffs the object of ridicule, humiliation, mental anguish, and emotional and physical distress, loss of reputation, goodwill, and standing in the community."

They also filed a motion for an injunction to prevent further distribution of the film until their scenes were excised or reedited so they didn't appear racist or misogynistic. Los Angeles Superior Court judge Joseph Biderman denied the request, ruling that "in order to obtain a preliminary injunction, a party must show (a) reasonable probability of success on the merits. In this case, the court finds that plaintiffs have failed to meet their burden of proof."

The two Alabama etiquette instructors also filed suits. Kathie B. Martin, who was shown photos of Borat's well-hung "son," told *Newsweek,* "I would've liked my fifteen minutes of fame in this life to have been for something more worthwhile than an R-rated movie." Her attorney tried drumming up a class action suit by seeking out other participants who wanted to sue.

Cindy Streit, proprietor of Etiquette Training Service, hired attorney Gloria Allred, who demanded an investigation of Baron Cohen's methods by the California Attorney General's Office for possible California Unfair Trade Practices Act violations. Allred claimed the filmmakers fraudulently told Ms. Streit she was participating in a documentary for Belarus television only. For her pain and suffering at being humiliated in front of her friends when Borat presented his bag of feces, the lawsuit called for a percentage of the film's profits.

One of Streit's dinner companions, Sarah Moseley, says,

"I went to the dinner party thinking I was there to talk about Christian values and my missionary friends who work in Kazakhstan. We were told we were meeting a diplomat who was interested in learning about southern hospitality. It was all lies. The whole way it was set up was totally deceptive.

"Cindy worked so hard to welcome this man and make him feel at home. It is so sad that a man of such talent would use that talent to hurt and humiliate people. I am sick of apologizing for what Baron Cohen has done in this disgusting film."

The pastor's wife, Sally Speaker, fumed to the *Sunday Mirror*: "Lives have been ruined by his comedy. I realize some people will watch the movie and find it funny, but for the people who were duped into appearing what happened was anything but humorous.

"It was horrible. Every time we thought he had done his worst, his behaviour would escalate. We thought he was from a foreign country, so we gave him the benefit of the doubt. But when the black prostitute arrived, we knew it was time to leave."

Her husband, minister Cary Speaker, says they have no intention of suing Baron Cohen even though he believes "the release forms were not worth the paper they were written on."

Media and international law attorney Mark Stephens, who was asked by 20th Century Fox to represent the studio when Kazakhstan was threatening litigation, says,

"The old adage 'where there's a hit, there's a writ' was never more apposite than in relation to *Borat*." He explains that the basis for the lawsuits was a lack of informed consent: "A look at the standard release used on the movie shows that the film is described as *a* 'documentary-style film. It is understood that the producer hopes to reach a young adult audience by using entertaining content and formats.' "

According to Stephens, everyone who appeared in the film was paid an appearance fee of $2,000 and "consented to, among other things: intrusion (such as any allegedly offensive behavior or questioning or any invasion of privacy); false light (such as any allegedly false or misleading portrayal of the participant); infliction of emotional distress (whether allegedly intentional or negligent); breach of any alleged contract (whether oral or written); allegedly deceptive business or trade practices; defamation (such as false statements made on film); violations of the Lanham Act (such as false or misleading statements or statements or suggestions about the Participant in relation to the film or the participant); fraud (such as . . . deception or surprise about the film or this consent agreement."

But perhaps the most important, and savvy, clause in the release is the one that says any claim must be brought in the State of New York—a state that Stephens says gives a "high level of constitutional protection . . . to satirical speech."

In October 2006, the European Center for Antiziganism Research, an advocate against discrimination against

Gypsies, filed a complaint with prosecutors in Hamburg, Germany, accusing Baron Cohen of defamation and inciting violence against the ethnic group, which violated Germany's anti-discrimination law.

In related news, the Russian Federal Agency for Culture and Cinematography banned the movie a month later because "it could offend viewers in relation to certain ethnic groups and religions."

Not to be outdone, the entire population of Glod,* the backwater Romanian Gypsy village that posed as Borat's Kazakhstan hometown, also attempted to bring a $30 million lawsuit against Baron Cohen for portraying them as "savages." In a suit filed in New York, the villagers demanded $5 million to improve their school and infrastructure—by such means as installing indoor plumbing and electricity—and another $25 million in humanitarian aid. On top of that, they asked the court that the villagers be compensated for their roles in the film.

The residents, who scrape out a living by selling scrap iron and farming small plots of land, have accused the production of tricking them into believing they were participating in a documentary about poverty.

"We were all set to go to Kazakhstan but we found that the people from Kazakhstan looked nothing like Borat," Mazer says. "We went to [Glod] and in exchange for letting us film we bought them a pig. It was actually the pig which

---

*The literal translation of Glod is "mud."

you see Borat introducing and then later eating. It was a great day filming."

It was reported that the film's producers gave the town $10,000 to pay for new computers for the local school. The residents denied it and the London tabloids had a field day trumpeting Glod's tales of woe. In a *Sunday Mail* article, Claudia Luca said, "We now realize they only came here because we are poorer than anyone else. . . . They never told us what they were doing but took advantage of our misfortune and poverty. They made us look like savages, why would anyone do that?"

Luca, who refers to Sacha as the "ugly, tall, moustachioed American man," admits the production team

> paid my family [forty-five dollars] for four full days. They were nice and friendly, but we could not understand a single word they were saying.
>
> We endured it because we are poor and badly needed the money, but now we realize we were cheated and taken advantage of in the worst way. All those things they said about us in the film are terribly humiliating. They said we drink horse urine and sleep with our own kin. You say it's comedy, but how can someone laugh at that?

The village has around one thousand residents and it was reported only four have steady employment in nearby towns, the majority living off of government subsidies. Nicu Tudorache, the man who at the end of the film is seen wearing a fist-shaped dildo as a prosthetic hand, was not remotely amused when told what the object's true purpose was. "This is disgusting," he angrily told the *Sunday Mail*. "They conned us into doing all these things and never told us anything about what was going on. They made us look like primitives, like uncivilized savages."

*Borat* writer Peter Baynham admits the dildo was initially a throwaway comic bit that took on a life of its own. "You think, *Okay, so we're shooting this bit with these gay people tomorrow, so let's have a rubber arm in the scene*," he says. "Later on, [Borat's] naked, chasing his partner down the corridor with the rubber arm. . . . It's hard, in a film like this, to keep that stuff in. You're obsessing, *Oh, we've got to keep the rubber arm because it'll be used in the hotel and then it'll be on the guy's arm at the end.* And production people are just thinking, *Oh, God . . .*"

Nicu says he agreed to participate after

> someone from the council said these Americans need a man with no arm for some scenes. I said yes but I never imagined the whole country, or even the whole world, will see me in the cinemas ridiculed in this way.
>
> Our region is very poor, and everyone is trying hard to get out of this misery. It is outrageous to exploit people's misfortune like this to

laugh at them. We are now coming together and will try to hire a lawyer and take legal action for being cheated and exploited. We are simple folk and don't know anything about these things, but I have faith in God and justice.

Hopefully, not American justice—a federal judge in New York dismissed Glod's suit, ruling the case did not have enough merit to go forward as then filed. The plaintiffs needed to present specific instances of how exactly they were misled.

Through it all, 20th Century Fox maintained their releases would hold up in court. And when pressed, most of those shown in the film admit they did not read the documents closely . . . if at all.

Ron Miller, who attended a formal dinner for Borat in Natchez, Mississippi, that did not make it into the film, says, "We have no idea what we signed." Even though Miller says he and the other guests felt "emotionally raped," he has no desire to sue. "Why be made a fool of twice?"

Sacha finds all the after-the-fact backpedaling an exercise in trying to save face. "This wasn't *Candid Camera*," he points out. "There were two large cameras in the room. I don't buy the argument that, 'oh, I wouldn't have acted so racist or anti-Semitic if I'd known this film was being shown in America.' That's no excuse."

In December 2006, Baron Cohen was nominated for two Golden Globe Awards for Best Actor and Best Picture in the Musical/Comedy category. "I have been trying to let Borat know this great news, but for the last four hours both of Kazakhstan's telephones have been engaged," Sacha joked. "Eventually Premier Nazarbayev answered and said he would pass on the message."

Although the film lost out to *Dreamgirls,* Sacha won the acting award. But when he got up to accept, he started his acceptance speech on a seemingly somber note.

"I want to thank the Hollywood Foreign Press [Association]. And I just want to say this movie was a life-changing experience. I saw some amazing, beautiful, invigorating parts of America. But I saw some dark parts of America. An ugly side of America. A side of America that rarely sees the light of day. . . ."

As the audience braced for a lecture on racism, Sacha delivered his punch line.

"I refer, of course, to the anus and testicles of my costar Ken Davitian. Ken . . . when I was in that scene, and I stared down and saw your two wrinkled Golden Globes on my chin, I thought to myself, *I'd better win a bloody award for this.*"

Davitian, who had not been invited to the awards ceremony but was given a last-minute ticket by a member of the Hollywood Foreign Press Association, held up a wine bottle in salute and chugged. "I was anticipating being on the list of thank-yous," he said later, "but not that."

After thanking his writers, director, producer, brother, stylist, and fiancée, Baron Cohen ended by thanking "every American who has not sued me so far."

Two months later, the writing team was nominated for an Academy Award. Even though they lost, Dan Mazer saw it as an otherworldly accomplishment. "It's an absolutely incredible thing, that a man who dangles his testicles in another man's face can be looked at for an Oscar nomination in the same film. But Sacha's ability to straddle that line is testament to his ability to range from sophisticated to puerile."

Baron Cohen says the nominations and awards were unexpected icing, but that they were the last thing on his mind when they set out to film the movie. "You make it because you want to make the funniest film possible and you want to make something that's satirical as well. And you want to make your friends laugh and you want to make your fans laugh. I'm just happy to get a couple of nominations and I'll take that and return to England."

Except Hollywood beckoned him to stay. After a multi-studio bidding war, Baron Cohen signed a reported $13 million deal with Universal for the rights to his next movie, making him the highest-paid actor in Britain. The contract also guarantees him 15 percent of the box office.

The question is, is it even possible for Sacha to ever go undercover again? *Ali G* producer Andrew Newman believes Sacha will adapt. While acknowledging that "Ali G and

Borat . . . have a built-in self-destruct mode," Newman stresses that "[Sacha] is a proper, funny actor. He does not only have to do hoaxing people."

Which is why, Baron Cohen says, his next movie may or may not be scripted and may or may not feature Bruno. But all indications are Borat, like Ali G, will be retired, at least for the time being. "I think it's going to be impossible to have him operate in the way he used to," Sacha says. "He might be going to live in a very obscure part of Kazakhstan where it's hard to contact him."

After living for so many years with Bruno, Borat, and Ali G, Sacha has other characters he'd like to develop. But he knows that he will never have the anonymity to make a film quite like *Borat* again, "which is a shame. . . . I'm just really looking forward to starting to do movies on set."

His first projects after the Borat juggernaut were *Madagascar 2* and Tim Burton's film adaptation of Stephen Sondheim's *Sweeney Todd*. In the film, Baron Cohen plays the corrupt barber Signor Adolfo Pirelli, whose blackmail attempt pushes Sweeney (Johnny Depp) into his murderous spree. According to *The Sun* in London, Sacha will be rapping his songs instead of singing them.

"Pirelli is a notoriously demanding role with some difficult songs," the paper quoted an unnamed source on the set as saying. "Any professional singer would struggle. So Sacha has been told to go for a rap style. There was never any question of Sacha being axed from the movie.

He is going to do a fantastic job. But he couldn't cut it with the singing. His voice was too low."

Baron Cohen's longtime collaborator, Dan Mazer, also signed a deal with Universal to write and make his directorial debut on an original comedy he is working on.

"Things that are genuinely funny are pretty rare in this world, and even rarer in Hollywood," says Mazer, who continues to live full-time in London. "For whatever reason, we seem to have smacked a nerve by making something that was truly funny. Having produced and cowritten what is turning out to be a two-hundred-million-dollar comedy has brought good fortune."

For Ken Davitian, too. He has been cast in the big-screen version of *Get Smart* as a KAOS villain. The film stars Steve Carell as Maxwell Smart, along with The Rock, Anne Hathaway, and Alan Arkin. "It's my first film that is with so many big people," Davitian notes. "I'm a day player who has finally made it."

It's his first experience of not having to audition. "People are calling . . . 'We want you.' This has the potential to change my life" but not to go to his head. "I'm older . . . and getting famous in the later years, I'm pretty well balanced. I'm finally starting to do what I love to do and I'm having a great time."

Hopefully, Baron Cohen will find a similar equilibrium and comfort zone as he balances fame and celebrity with his desire to maintain a private life, especially now that he and Fisher are starting a family. Or expanding the one they already have. A London paper reported that Sacha and Isla are already proud parents . . . of a blue-footed booby.* *The Mirror* says he adopted one of the blue-footed, goose-sized birds on her behalf as a Valentine's day gift.

"Although she doesn't strictly own the bird," the paper explained, "Isla is now deemed a 'proud parent' and Sacha will pay a monthly fee to pay for the booby's upkeep in the wild."

From Ali G to Borat to Bruno to the blue-footed booby, Sacha has a unique take on the world that has touched a comedic nerve—something that still amazes him. "The bizarre thing is that people actually came to see it. That first weekend, when I found out we were the most popular film in America, it was the most bizarre and overwhelming experience."

Dan Mazer views himself and Baron Cohen as pioneers. "We've helped craft what I think is this new and exciting art form and I think we're going to start to see lots of imitators now."

Sacha believes that's to be expected—and encouraged.

"That's what happens when you do something that's

---

*"Booby" comes from the Spanish word *bobo,* which means "stupid fellow." Naturally tame, the birds were easily caught by Spanish explorers, thus the name booby. You can adopt your own at secure.worldwildlife.org or at secure .gct.org.

new and fresh. That was really the challenge with this movie—it was an experiment. And weirdly enough, it was an experiment that worked. So if it gets copied, then I'm happy that it's a form of cinema that can continue."

WORKS CITED

AAP. "Fisher Crashes the Red Carpet." *The Sydney Morning Herald,* August 1, 2005.

Abcarian, Robin. "Borat Sidekick Is Less Recognizable with Clothes." *Los Angeles Times,* February 23, 2007.

"Affronted Feminist Naomi Wolf Takes a Bite out of 'Racist' Ali G." *The Sunday Times,* March 9, 2003.

Alderson, Andrew. "The Day Great Granny Did Her Ali G Rap at the Dinner Table." *The Telegraph,* April 7, 2002.

"Ali G Takes Home Spare Bafta." BBC News, May 16, 2001, at news.bbc.co.uk.

"Ali Goes Ivy League: 2004 Harvard University Commencement Speech." Posted at www.hbo.com/alig/harvard.html.

Ali, Lorraine. "'G' Hits the Funny Spot: Wazzup Wit Dis Ali G?" *Newsweek,* February 24, 2003.

Ansen, David. "Too Funny—Or Too Far?" *Newsweek,* November 13, 2006.

Armstrong, Stephen. "I'm Faster Than Britney Spears." *The Sunday Times,* October 1, 2006.

Bagenal, Flora, and John Harlow. "Borat Make Benefit Kazakh Tourist Boom." *The Sunday Times,* November 3, 2006.

Bamigboye, Baz. "Borat's a Cheeky Chap, but That's His Appeal." *Daily Mail,* May 26, 2006.

"Behind the Scenes: Randall Shelley." The Unofficial Borat Page, at www.boratonline.co.uk.

Born, Matt. "BBC Tightens Rule on Taste After Ali G Expletives." *Daily Mail,* April 25, 2002.

———."The Phoney, Cynical World of Ali G's Role Model." *Daily Mail,* June 9, 2006.

Bunbury, Stephanie. "Fishing for Trouble." *The Age,* August 7, 2005, at www
.theage.com/au.

Callan, Jessica, and Eva Simpson. "What's Da Deal, Ali?" *Daily Mirror,* March 22,
2002.

Callan, Jessica, Eva Simpson, and Polly Graham. "Madge Snubs Sacha's Movie."
*Daily Mirror,* May 15, 2001.

"Can Borat Be Sued by the 'I Kiss You!' Guy?" Electronic News Network,
November 3, 2006, celebs.electronicnewsnetwork.com/sacha-cohen/.

CBC Arts. "Daughter of Kazakhstan's President Defends Borat." CBC Radio-
Canada, April 21, 2006, at ww.cbc.ca.

CBS News. "'Ali G' Comedian Riles Rodeo Crowd." January 14, 2005, at www
.cbsnews.com.

Celebrity Mound press release, November 25, 2006, at www.celebritymound
.com.

Clarke, Jon, and Glenys Roberts. "Is It Coz I Is Welsh?" *Daily Mail,* April 20,
2002.

Cohen, Nadia. "What Will Julie Say Now, Ali?" *Daily Mail,* February 25, 2002.

Cohen, Rich. "Hello! It's Sexy Time!" *Vanity Fair,* December 2006.

Conlan, Tara. "Millions Hear Ali G Swear on Air." *Daily Mail,* February 19,
2002.

Cooper, Glenda. "The Secret World of Sacha B." *Daily Mail,* February
19, 2002.

Crus, Clarissa. "Maid of Honor: Scene-Stealer Isla Fisher Gets Clap-Happy."
*Entertainment Weekly,* July 15, 2005.

Cukier, Kenneth Neil. "No Joke." *Foreign Affairs,* December 28, 2005, at www
.foreignaffairs.org.

Culliford, Graeme. "Movie Has Ruined Me Says Supper Club's Host." *Sunday
Mirror,* November 19, 2006.

Daniel, Robert. "*Dog Bites Man* creator Dan Mazer." SuicideGirls.com, July 25,
2006, at www.suicidegirls.com.

"Darren's Girl Is a Great Lover . . . But Only with Lights Off!" *The People,*
December 27, 1998.

Davies, Mike. "At the Movies: Shell-Shocked Mike Davies Comes Face to Face
with Me Julie, Ali G's Long-Suffering Girlfriend." *The Birmingham Post,*
March 23, 2003.

Dee, Johnny. "The Real Borat." *The Guardian,* October 28, 2006.

Dewar, Angela. "The First Eleven." *Sunday Mail.* October 17, 1999.

DiOrio, Carl. "'Borat' Judge: No Suit for You." *The Hollywood Reporter,*
December 12, 2006.

E&P staff. "Take That, Borat: Kazakhstan Runs 4-Page Ad Section in *N.Y.*

*Times.*" *Editor & Publisher,* November 28, 2005, reposted at www .freerepublic.com.

Edwards, David. "Wham Pam Kazakhstan." *Daily Mirror,* November 3, 2006.

Eglash, Rush. "Despite 'Borat,' Kazakhs Seek Stronger Ties with Israel." *The Jerusalem Post,* November 6, 2006.

Elkin, Michael. "Ali Babble; Is Sacha Baron Cohen the Bad Boy of Jewish Comics?" *Jewish Exponent,* October 14, 2004.

Elliott, John. "Borat Goes on the US Offensive (Very)." *The Sunday Times,* June 8, 2006.

Elsworth, Catherine. "The Joke Is on the Racists, Says Relaxed Borat." *The Telegraph,* November 17, 2006.

Farrell, Stephen. "Ali G Escapes 'Suicide' Bullet." *The Times,* December 31, 2002.

Fischer, Paul. "Aussie Actress Isla Fisher on the *Wedding Crashers* and Hollywood." *Film Monthly.com,* June 15, 2005.

Fitzpatrick, Rob. "You Dirty Borat!" *The Guardian,* October 28, 2006.

Fleming, Michael. "Borat's Pal Will Direct U Comedy." *Variety,* December 13, 2006.

Freydkin, Donna. "The Many Faces of Sacha Baron Cohen." *USA Today,* October 27, 2006.

"From the Sublime to the Ridicule." *The Telegraph,* March 12, 2001.

Fryer, Jane. "Ali G's Back-Room Friend." *The Scotsman,* April 4, 2003.

Glenn, Joshua. "Surprise Kazakh." *The Boston Globe,* November 27, 2005.

Goldstein, Patrick. "Borat Gives Cohen License to Be Outrageous." *Los Angeles Times,* January 9, 2007.

Gordon, Devin. "Behind the Schemes." *Newsweek,* October 16, 2006.

————."The Brain Behind Borat." *Newsweek,* November 13, 2006.

Gorov, Lynda. "As an Over-the-Top Bridesmaid, She Comes Crashing into the Spotlight." *The Boston Globe,* July 24, 2005.

Green, Lucia. "The Day I Nearly Died." *Sunday Mirror,* September 28, 1997.

Gross, Terry. *Fresh Air from WHYY.* January 4, 2007.

Hammack, Laurance. "Rodeo in Salem Gets Unexpected Song Rendition." *The Roanoke Times,* January 9, 2005, at www.roanoke.com.

Hancock, Louise. "Do I Manipulate Men? That's What They're For." *Sunday Mirror,* July 14, 2002.

"Harry Thompson: Founder Producer of 'Have I Got News for You.' " *The Independent,* November 9, 2005.

"Head Porter Saw Comic's Potential." *Cambridge Evening News,* November 9, 2006.

Heffernan, Virginia. "The Cheerful Confessions of Ali G, Borat and Bruno." *The New York Times,* July 15, 2004.

Henegan, Nick. "Kazakh's Fury over TV Sacha." *Daily Mirror,* September 20, 2004.

Horovitz, David. "In My Country There Is Problem—with Borat." *The Jerusalem Post,* December 1, 2006.

Idrissov, Erlan. "Offensive and Unfair, Borat's Antics Leave a Nasty Aftertaste." *The Guardian,* October 4, 2006.

Iley, Chrissy. "Chrissy Iley on Sacha Baron Cohen and Ali G." *The Scotsman,* April 6, 2002.

"I'm Ali G's Girl Julie; Tamzin Was First Choice for Movie Role but Had to Turn Down Old Pal Sacha." *Daily Record,* April 4, 2002.

"Interview with Dan Mazer, Producer of *Da Ali G Show.*" The Unofficial Borat Page, at www.boratonline.co.uk.

"Isla Fisher Tributes Her Work to Fiancé." NineMSN.com, September 11, 2006, at news.ninemsn.com.au.

"Isla Won't Be Borat's Girl." *The Sun,* October 16, 2006.

"It's Sacha Shame." *Daily Mirror.* November 12, 2005.

"Just Like a Real Wedding." *The Daily Telegraph,* August 3, 2005.

Kalman, Matthew. "Ali G Sleeps as Bullets Fly." *Daily Mail,* December 31, 2002.

Key, Ivor. "Has Ali G Gone Too Far?" *Daily Mail,* February 24, 2003.

King, Kiki, Eva Simpson, and Caroline Hedley. "Sacha Softy." *Daily Mirror,* November 3, 2005.

Kit, Borys. "Davitian Spies 'Smart' Role as KAOS Bad." *Hollywood Reporter,* March 5, 2007.

Koch, John. "The Brains Behind Borat." *Written By,* January 2007.

Koster, Olinka. "Ali G's Tacky Show." *Daily Mail,* March 21, 2002.

Lampert, Nicole. "Ali G Goes to Hollywood." *Daily News,* March 2, 2004.

———."Ali G in Anti-Semitic Storm." *Daily Mail,* August 20, 2004.

Lee-Potter, Lynda. "Who Can Find This Vile Man Amusing?" *Daily Mail,* February 20, 2002.

Leibovitz, Liel. "Did Ali G Go Too Far?" *The Jewish Week,* August 13, 2004.

Levy, Emanuel. "On the Road with Borat Sagdiyev." *The Jerusalem Post,* November 19, 2006.

Lillington, Alex. Interview with *School for Scoundrels* director Todd Phillips. FirstShowing.net, September 27, 2006.

Lindrea, Victoria. "Borat Creator Has the Final Word." BBC News, February 23, 2007, at news.bbc.co.uk.

Malins, Sue. "Soap Hunks Are Too Pretty for Me." *Daily Mirror,* July 11, 1996.

Marchese, David, and Willa Paskin. "What's Real in Borat?" *Salon.com,* November 10, 2006.

Marre, Oliver. "Sacha Baron Cohen: Our Man from Kazakhstan." *The Observer,* September 10, 2006.

McGurran, Aidan. "It's Wally G, Innit." *Daily Record,* January 20, 2000.

McVeigh, Karen. "Me Kelli Indahouse." Living, *The Scotsman,* March 13, 2002.

Meller, Henry. "Ali G in Da Doghouse." *Daily Mail,* January 19, 2005.

————."Exit Ali G Director, Fearing for His Life." *Daily Mail,* January 19, 2005.

Mendick, Robert. "Ali G Loses a Fan in the Queen Mother, William and Harry Reveal." *The Independent Sunday,* April 7, 2002.

Millar, John. "French Leave Made Me a Real Actress." *Daily Record,* June 20, 1998.

Miller, Harland. "Lord of the Bling." *The Guardian,* April 20, 2004.

Moore, Matthew. "Cohen Sued for 'Libelling Friend' on Ali G Show." *The Telegraph,* February 28, 2007.

Moran, Jonathan. "Fisher, Ali G 'to Wed Down Under.'" *The Sydney Morning Herald,* August 1, 2005.

More TV Land. "Sacha Baron Cohen." *Daily Mirror,* July 16, 2005.

Murray, Rebecca. "Isla Fisher Talks About Her Role in the Romantic Comedy *Wedding Crashers.*" About.com Hollywood Movies, at movies.about.com.

Myskow, Nina. "The Real Me: Isla Fisher." *Daily Mirror,* December 18, 1998.

News. "Grandma Did an Impression of Ali G." *Daily Mail,* April 7, 2002.

————."Kazakh President Arrives for Three-Day Visit Amid Borat Storm." *Daily Mail,* November 20, 2006.

Nicholl, Katie. "Ali G R.I.P. Star to Kill Off TV Creation as He Seeks Film Fame." *Sunday Mail,* September 21, 2003.

"No Time to Stall." *Cambridge Evening News,* October 5, 2004.

O'Connell, Jennifer. "Naomi Wolf." *Business Post,* March 30, 2003.

Page Six. "Pam Was In on Borat Joke." *New York Post,* November 8, 2006.

Pancevski, Bojan, and Carmiola Ionescu. "Borat Film 'Tricked' Poor Village Actor." *Sunday Mail,* November 11, 2006.

"Parents Are Horrified, but Their Kids Have Heard Much Worse." *Cambridge Evening News,* November 11, 2005.

Pattison, Georgina. "Those Ali G Moments." *The Birmingham Post,* March 31, 2000.

People & Places. "The Man Behind the Moustache: Sacha Baron Cohen." *Day to Day,* NPR, January 12, 2007.

Peppard, Alan. "Ali G Goes a Few Rounds with Boxing Class." *Dallas Morning News,* July 25, 2005.

Phillips, Michael. "Broken Reel a Cause for Comedy." *Chicago Tribune,* September 9, 2006.

Pond, Steve. "Comedy for the Ages." *USA Weekend,* November 5, 2006.

Radosh, Daniel. "Department of Foreign Relations: The Borat Docrine." *The New Yorker,* September 20, 2004.

Rayner, Gordon. "The Unanswered Questions About What Really Went on at Barrymore's Home That Night." *Daily Mail,* June 15, 2007.

Rayner, Jay. "Mutha of Invention." *The Observer,* February 24, 2002.

Reid, Dixie. "Going Wild." *The Sacramento Bee,* May 25, 2005.

"Reporters Without Borders Raps Censorship of UK Comedian's 'Borat' Website." Reporters Without Borders, December 14, 2005, at www.rsf.org.

Reuters. "Now Gypsies Want Borat Banned." *The Sydney Morning Herald,* October 18, 2007.

Rollings, Grant. "Comedy Genius Sacha Opens Up." *The Sun,* November 22, 2006.

Rottenberg, Josh. "The Village Idiot Genius." *Entertainment Weekly,* October 20, 2006.

Rubin, Harriet. "Boooorrriinng!!!" *Fast Company,* May 2000.

"Sacha Baron Cohen." *People,* November 29, 2004.

Sauer, Abram. "Borat vs. Kazakhstan." BrandChannel.com, October 30, 2006, at www.brandchannel.com.

Sayid, Ruki. "It's Ali in de Mirror." *Daily Mirror,* January 12, 2000.

Scott, James. "How to Talk Nice." *Daily Mirror,* March 9, 2002.

Scott, James, and Charlie Bain. "Madonna: The Big Day." *Daily Mirror,* December 22, 2000.

Scott, Kirsty. "Sexist, Anti-Semitic and Homophobic, Comic's New Character Set for Stardom." *The Guardian,* September 29, 2006.

Shaikh, Thair. "Staines Names Ali G as Its Ambassador." *The Telegraph,* March 30, 2002.

Simpson, Eva, and Caroline Hedley. "Borat Am Enjoying the Londons Ladies!" *Daily Mirror,* October 26, 2006.

Simpson, Richard. "Ali G Is King for a Night with a Change of Tacky." *The Evening Standard,* March 21, 2002.

————."When Ali G Is Your Little Brother . . . Madonna Comes to Tea and You Let Guy Win at Chess." *The Evening Standard,* November 8, 2001.

Smith, Emily. "Borat Spanked by Angry Yank." *Daily News,* November 13, 2006.

Stein, Joel. "Borat Make Funny Joke on Idiot Americans! High-Five!" *Time,* November 6, 2006.

Stephens, Mark. "Jagshemash! I No Like You, I Sue You." *The Times,* November 24, 2006.

Strauss, Neil. "As Clueless as He Wants to Be." *The New York Times,* February 3, 2003.

————."The Man Behind the Mustache." *Rolling Stone,* November 14, 2006.

Sullivan, Andy. "White House Gates Shut to 'Kazakh Reporter' Comic." Reuters. September 29, 2006.

Tookey, Christopher. "Ali G in Da House." *Daily Mail,* March 20, 2002.

————."Borat Is Rude, and Crude—He's Also Hilarious." *Daily Mail,* March 11, 2006.

Tugend, Tom. "Dirty Jokes but a Kosher Comedian." *The Jerusalem Post,* August 9, 2006.

TV & Showbiz. "Ali G Rapped over Slang Word." *Daily Mail,* January 15, 2001.

————."Ali G to Make His Debut on US TV." *Daily Mail,* January 10, 2003.

————. "Ali G: 'I Is Marrying Me Julie.'" *Daily Mail,* March 4, 2004.

————. "Borat Star's Secret Cheesy Local TV Past." *Daily Mail,* November 27, 2006.

————."Borat Success Sparks Million Dollar Bidding War for Rights to Next Film." *Daily Mail,* October 27, 2006.

————."Everyone Knows 'Borat'—But Who Is Sacha?" *Daily Mail,* November 10, 2006.

————."Pin-up Pam's Role in *Borat* Angered Husband Kid Rock." *Daily Mail,* November 29, 2006.

————."Spoof Kazakhstani Reporter Borat Sparks White House Crisis Talks." *Daily Mail,* September 29, 2006.

————."Wood: Ali G Show Horrible, Innit." *Daily Mail,* February 1, 2005.

Tweedie, Neil, and Thomas Harding. "The Polite Little Swot Who Grew into Ali G." *The Telegraph,* March 8, 2002.

"Valley G's Wicked Welsh Rootz." BBC News, March 28, 2002, at news.bbc.co.uk.

Walker, Alexander. "Ali G in Da House." *The Evening Standard,* March 21, 2002.

Wapshott, Nicholas. "Oh, It's a Joke? America Struggles with Ali G." *The Times,* February 21, 2003.

"Warning: Ali G in Area Pranking People." *Dallas–Fort Worth Quick,* July 22, 2005.

Waxman, Sharon. "Equal-Opportunity Offender Plays Anti-Semitism for Laughs." *The New York Times,* September 7, 2006.

The Week. *National Review,* March 24, 2003.

Weiss Green, Elizabeth. "America's Best Colleges 2007" issue. *U.S. News & World Report,* 2007.

————. "South Carolina Reviewer Likes Borat; Frat Brother Likes His Mom." *U.S. News & World Report,* November 7, 2006.

Welkos, Robert W., and Mark Olsen. "Script for 'Borat' Surfaces Just in Time." *Los Angeles Times,* January 21, 2007.

# WORKS CITED

Whitaker, Thomas. "Ali G 'Nicked Jim's Cool Image.'" *The Sun*, March 20, 2002.

White, Donna. "We Woz Coonned by Ali G." *Sunday Mail*, April 2, 2000.

White, Roland. "Borat's Easy . . . Being Me Is Odd." *The Sunday Times*, January 21, 2007.

# INDEX

# INDEX

# INDEX

# INDEX